Seeing the
Solar System

Other Wiley Science Editions

Seeing the Solar System

Telescopic Projects, Activities, and Explorations in Astronomy

FRED SCHAAF

with illustrations by Doug Myers

Wiley Science Editions

JOHN WILEY & SONS, INC.

New York • Chichester • Brisbane • Toronto • Singapore

This publication is designed to provide accurate and authoritative information in regard to the subject matter covered. It is sold with the understanding that the publisher is not engaged in rendering legal, accounting or other professional service. If legal advice or other expert assistance is required, the services of a competent professional person should be sought. FROM A DECLARATION OF PRINCIPLES JOINTLY ADOPTED BY A COMMITTEE OF THE AMERICAN BAR ASSOCIATION AND A COMMITTEE OF PUBLISHERS.

Library of Congress Cataloging in Publication Data

Schaaf, Fred.
   Seeing the solar system ; telescopic projects, activities & explorations / Fred Schaaf ; with illustrations by Doug Myers.
     p. cm. — (Wiley science editions)
   Includes bibliographical references.
   ISBN 0-471-53070-0. — ISBN 0-471-53071-9 (pbk.)
   1. Astronomy projects—Popular works. 2. Telescopes—Popular works. 3. Astronomy—Observers' manuals. I. Title. II. Series.
   QB64.S4273 1991
   522'.2'078—dc20
                                                                   91-11049

Printed in the United States of America

10 9 8 7 6 5 4 3 2 1

Preface

This book is complete in itself. But it is also the second in what will be at least a trilogy. The first volume, published in 1990, is *Seeing the Sky*—a selection of astronomical activities for naked-eye observers. The book you now hold in your hands offers projects concerning the Sun, Moon, planets, and other bodies of our solar system for telescopic observers. The next book will also feature telescopic projects, but ones involving celestial objects beyond our solar system—stars of all kinds, star clusters, nebulas, galaxies, and quasars.

All three of these books are intended to be suitable for use by everyone from the beginning to the quite advanced observer, by the bright junior high school student as well as the adult amateur astronomer. A fairly small telescope will suffice for most of activities in the telescopic books. The present book does contain some projects that are devoted largely to elementary facts and basic observations, but in most cases I think these projects are presented in a manner that even the veteran skywatcher will benefit from reviewing.

In the previous book, *Seeing the Sky*, I was anxious to present projects that were outstandingly original. That was easier to do with naked-eye observations because they have been neglected so much in recent years. After the completion of that book, however, I realized that organizing *all* the important telescopic observations that can be made of various celestial objects in the format of projects like those of the first book would itself be original. I am not aware of anyone who has attempted this with anything like comprehensiveness or for adult amateur astronomers (though not only for adult amateur astronomers).

PREFACE

This book covers so much territory, with hundreds of individual inquiries for the observer to pursue, that it scarcely needs (and would be unwise to try including) the whole vast additional realm of possibilities opened by advanced astrophotography or the use of other instruments with the telescope. But there are other reasons for this book to concentrate on projects requiring the telescope only. Not everyone—not even all high schools or colleges, let alone all individuals beginning the study of astronomy—can immediately afford much equipment beyond the basic telescope. In this book, I have made comment on the use of various filters for planetary observation because they can be so helpful and are not prohibitively expensive. Otherwise, the book assumes only a basic telescope—and not necessarily a large one—is in the reader's possession. And, as for the proper use and care of a telescope or the advantages and drawbacks of different kinds of telescope, these are certainly matters that require a lot of explanation, but they certainly fall outside the province and aim of this book. See the "Sources of Information" section for ideas about where to turn for this advice.

In conclusion, I wish to encourage readers to write to me with any comments or suggestions, and especially with any observational results elicited by the reading of this book. You can write to me in care of Wiley Science Editions, John Wiley & Sons, Inc., 605 Third Avenue, New York, NY 10158.

My sincerest hope about this book is that it will be used. Make acquaintance with the fellow worlds of our solar system—not just on the page but in your telescope. I do not think you will find it easy to get over the polar ice caps of Mars, to forget the rings of Saturn, or to let go of the lunar crater Copernicus—not once you have looked upon these things with some depth of knowledge and with a purpose.

Fred Schaaf

Note on Telescopes, Transparency and "Seeing," and Light Pollution

Telescopes. In the preface, I explained that this book is not a guide to telescope selection, use, or care. The reader is directed to the "Sources of Information" section for suggested reading on the topic. But a few elementary points on telescopes may be mentioned here.

The three most important types of telescopes are the *reflector*, the *refractor*, and the *catadioptric*. The reflector uses mirrors and the refractor uses lenses, while the catadioptric employs both reflective and refractive elements. The most popular type of reflector is the Newtonian; the most popular catadioptric is the Schmidt–Cassegrain. For the lunar and planetary observing with which most of this book is concerned, the large focal ratios (ratio of mirror or lens focal length to its width) of refractors and of some reflectors are most desirable. A good Schmidt–Cassegrain will be sufficient for such observations, however. And four of the activities concern comets—objects for which the lower magnifications and wider fields of a "faster" (smaller focal ratio) telescope are most needed. A comet observer will often be using a small Newtonian RFT (rich-field telescope) or refractor.

The two most important types of telescope mountings are the *equatorial* and the *altazimuth*. A special form of the latter, the Dobsonian mounting, has become popular in the past decade for "deep-sky" observing. But for observing fine details on the Moon and planets, a clock drive to compensate for Earth's rotation becomes more important—and such a drive must be used with an equatorial mount. (Adapting an altazimuth for a clock drive is possible but requires considerable modifications.)

The quality of the eyepieces, or *oculars*, used with a telescope can make a great difference in what you see. Also very important is the proper alignment, or *collimation*, of the optical elements. The finest telescope will not perform very well with poor eyepieces and may be positively wasted if it is not kept at least fairly well collimated.

Transparency and "Seeing." There is more to good observing conditions than a cloud-free sky. The atmosphere's degree of freedom from moisture and dust is called *transparency*. The atmosphere's degree of freedom from turbulence is called "seeing."

Some kinds of astronomical observations demand good transparency; others, good seeing. Any observation that requires glimpsing faint objects is best tried when the transparency is good, for the light from celestial objects is scattered away by moisture and dust in the air. Any observation that requires sharp images is best tried when the seeing is good, for the steadier the atmosphere is (the less turbulent) the sharper your view should be. Most lunar and planetary viewing does not require excellent transparency because we are dealing with bright objects. In fact, in some cases they are so bright against the night sky that twilight or daytime observation or use of filters may be in order. On the other hand, the fine detail and subtle contrasts of features on the surface or in the atmosphere of these distant worlds demand good seeing.

Light Pollution. Some of the planets are so bright that telescopic observation of them is not really hindered by brilliant moonlight or city lights. The other planets, the planetary satellites, the asteroids, the meteors, and, most especially, the comets are a different story, however. Nowadays, anyone who wants to view them faces the same critical problem that confronts almost all observations, naked-eye or telescopic, of anything beyond our solar system—the problem of *light pollution*.

Light pollution is usually defined as excessive or misdirected artificial outdoor lighting. It results from inferior lighting fixtures and practices that do more than rob us of our view of the universe. Light pollution costs all of us money (several billion dollars a year in the United States alone) and wastes energy, forcing millions of extra tons of coal and barrels of oil to be burned each year—a significant contribution to air pollution, acid rain, and greenhouse warming. The glare from poor lighting fixtures greatly reduces traffic safety and certainly does not help provide greater security against crime.

Since light pollution hurts all of us, there is real hope that the movement to reduce it will eventually succeed. I urge every reader of this book to help restore our generation's view of the heavens, and to save the next generation's, by learning more about the problem and its solutions and by sharing that information with others. The essential way to begin is to consult the central clearinghouse for light pollution information and advice, the International Dark-sky Association (IDA). For information, write to:

IDA
3545 North Stewart
Tucson, AZ 85716

Note on the Measurement of Time, Position, Angular Distance, and Brightness in Astronomy

The following concepts are not necessary to know for most activities in this book; for a few activities, however, they are very important.

Time. Universal Time (UT) is 24-hour time, essentially the same as Greenwich Mean Time (GMT). The day in UT begins at midnight in the time zone of England's Greenwich meridian. In the United States, Local Standard Time is 5 (Eastern Standard Time [EST]), 6 (Central Standard Time [CST]), 7 (Mountain Standard Time [MST]), and 8 (Pacific Standard Time [PST]) hours behind UT. Thus, 10h UT on January 18 would be 5:00 A.M. EST, and 4h UT on January 18 would be 11:00 P.M. EST on January 17.

Position. A system of celestial coordinates sometimes referred to in this book is that of right ascension (RA) and declination. On the celestial sphere of the heavens, with its equator and poles directly over those of Earth, RA and declination are similar to longitude and latitude, respectively, on Earth. RA is not measured in degrees west or east of the Greenwich meridian, however, but in 24 "hours" (containing "minutes" and "seconds" of angular measure), which run east from the 0^h line of RA. That line goes through the vernal equinox point in the sky (where the Sun is located in the heavens as spring begins). Declination is measured in degrees, minutes, and seconds, like latitude, but declinations north of the celestial equator are preceded by a plus sign ($+$) and those south of the celestial equator by a minus sign ($-$).

NOTE ON MEASUREMENT

Angular Distance. From horizon to zenith is 90 degrees (out of the 360 degrees around the entire heavens above and below the horizon). The Moon and Sun appear about 0.5 degree wide. Your fist at arm's length is about 10 degrees wide.

Brightness. In astronomy, brightness is measured by *magnitude*. Originally, all naked-eye stars were categorized in six classes of brightness, from first magnitude (brightest) to sixth magnitude (faintest). In modern times, the scale has been extended to zero and to negative magnitudes for very bright objects and to much higher numbers for objects so faint that they require optical aid to see. Decimals are used between two magnitudes: A star midway in brightness between magnitudes 1.0 and 2.0 is 1.5 (the magnitude 1.5 star is dimmer than magnitude 1.0—the lower the magnitude, the brighter the object). A difference of 1 magnitude means one object is about 2.512 times brighter than another. This is because it was considered useful to set a 5-magnitude difference equal to 100 times—2.512 (actually 2.5118. . .) multiplied by itself 5 times is 100.

Metric Conversions. This book uses both miles and kilometers. To convert from kilometers to miles, multiply the figure by 0.6214. To convert from miles to kilometers, multiply the figure by 1.609.

Contents

MOON, SUN, AND ECLIPSES　　1

CONTENTS

PLANETS 61

CONTENTS

COMETS, ASTEROIDS, AND METEORS   163

MOON, SUN, AND ECLIPSES

1.

General Observations of the Moon

Compare the visibility of topographic lunar features near the terminator to that of features far from it. Observe the first appearance and then increasing prominence of rays from lunar craters as the Moon waxes and their decreasing prominence as it wanes. Study the foreshortening of lunar craters and other features near the limb. Note the changes in the amount of foreshortening caused by libration over the course of many nights.

Everyone who owns a telescope knows the awe of that first look at the Moon. Perhaps no sight in all of nature presents us with a greater impression of brightness, hugeness, and glorious complexity.

The only problem is that for beginning lunar observers the complexity can also be bewildering. Since a 6-inch telescope can reveal craters down to about a mile across and linear formations much thinner, something like a million features are visible with such an instrument. Far more confusing than mere numbers is the changing appearance of the features caused by the fairly rapidly changing angle of sunlight on the Moon due to the Moon's orbiting and the slower waggings of the Moon's face (both side-to-side and up-and-down) called *libration*.

What, then, is the best way to start the seemingly monumental task (and truly monumental adventure) of learning the features on the Moon? Our first activity in this book does not even call for learning individual features. It calls for studying how libration and the progress of the lunar day change the appearance of all lunar features.

After your initial marvel at the brilliance and hugeness of the Moon and the mind-boggling number of craters and other features on its face, you may next notice that the general visibility of these features varies according to two factors. One is how far the feature is from the line separating light and dark (day and night) on the Moon. The other factor is how far the feature is from the edge of the earthward-pointing side of the Moon, the edge of the disk of Moon we observe.

The line separating day and night on the Moon (or on any world) is the *terminator*. At any phase except Full Moon and New Moon, you can view the terminator with a telescope and see in a moment that the topographic features near the terminator all appear much sharper and more

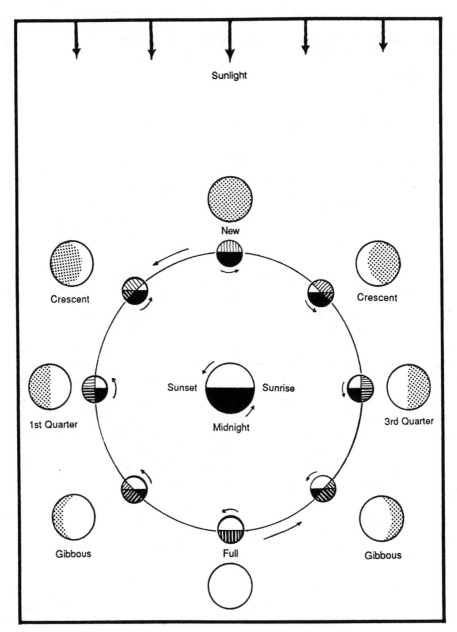

Figure 1 Phases of the Moon.

prominent than those far from it. The reason for this is the role the angle of sunlight plays in producing shadows. Parts of the Moon far from the terminator are shined on by the Sun from high in their sky. These appear "washed-out" from being bathed almost all over with sunlight (little or no shadow). On the other hand, parts of the Moon near the terminator see a Sun that is low in their sky. Features in these parts are thus lit on one side and prominently shadowed on the other. Even a very small or very shallow crater not visible most of the time is easily visible now because it stands out in such strong relief.

The exception to this rule is lunar features that are not topographic—in other words, that do not represent variations in altitude. The outstanding example is the long streaks of brighter lunar dust that radiate out from certain of the younger craters on the Moon. These *rays* are only visible when the Sun shines down from on high upon them—when they are far from the terminator. Near Full Moon, several of the great systems of rays (especially that of the crater Tycho, rather near the southern edge of the Moon) are impossible not to see in a telescope. Watch how these seem to fade magically from view as the Moon's phase decreases.

Almost as obvious as the effect of the terminator on a lunar feature's appearance is the effect of its distance from the edge, or *limb*, of the Moon. You will see no round craters near the limb, not because they are really not round, but because they look elliptical (finally almost linear) due to foreshortening from the angle at which we are seeing them. Some of the Moon's largest craters appear as little more than lines because we are having to view them from such a shallow angle.

Now, although lunar features are not always lit the same, at least we would not have trouble recognizing them by their shape—more or less foreshortened due to their distance from the limb—if it were not for the fact that the amount of foreshortening changes. And of course that can only occur if the Moon is not keeping quite exactly the same face toward us but rather tilting its face slightly up and down, right and left. This phenomenon, libration, results from several different causes—or, more properly, we should say that there are several different kinds. (They are discussed in detail in Activity 9.)

For our purposes in the present activity, it is sufficient for us to merely observe the existence of libration and know generally what its effects are over the course of weeks of observing. You can do this by studying a prominent feature near the Moon's limb for a number of nights and seeing how its apparent distance from the limb and its apparent shape both seem to change. The largest feature good for this purpose is a small, isolated "sea," Mare Crisium. See Figure 2. Even the naked eye can notice its changes in apparent shape and position on the waxing Moon.

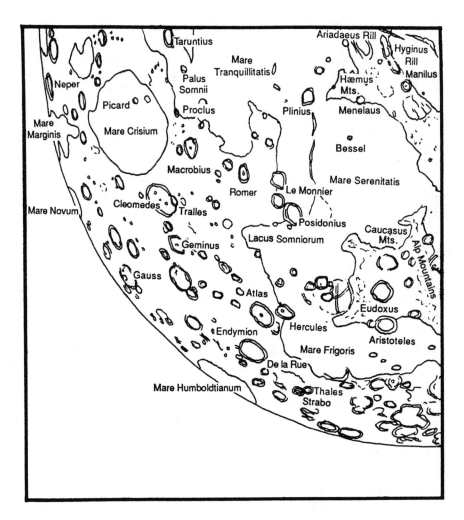

Figure 2 Moon Quadrant 1—Northeast Quadrant. South is up and east is left, as in most telescopes.

Questions

1. How does the appearance of lunar craters and mountains near the terminator differ from the appearance of those far from it? Do you notice any such features that were prominent near the terminator become lost from your view in the brightly lit part of the Moon a few nights later?

2. When are the ray-systems of various craters most prominent? How many nights before and after this time are they entirely lost from view?

3. How close to the Moon's limb can you detect various kinds of lunar features, despite their severe foreshortening? What are the extremes in distance from the limb for various features during the course of a few weeks of libration? Do you see any features lost at the limb when this area gets tilted away?

2.

Tour of the Moon—Evening Crescent to First Quarter

Identify major lunar features as the terminator goes past them on various nights from the time the waxing Moon is a slender evening crescent until the time it reaches First Quarter. Write down your impressions and sketch the appearance of features such as Mare Crisium, Langrenus, Vendelinus, Petavius, Proclus, Fracastorius, the Rheita Valley, Atlas and Hercules, Aristoteles and Eudoxus, Theophilus and its neighbors, the Altai Scarp, Hipparchus and Albategnius, Aristillus and Autolycus, and the Alps and Alpine Valley.

If you understand the basic astronomical factors affecting the visibility of features on the Moon—preferably by actually performing Activity 1—you are ready to start learning individual features. Perhaps the most natural plan for taking a first tour is to harness the lunar phases themselves by following the terminator across the Moon's face during the course of a month. This will be the plan in the present activity and the next two.

Figures 2 through 5 are basic maps of the quadrants of the Moon's earthward face. Note that east on the Moon (thus on our maps and in all of the text that follows) is officially the direction from which a person on the Moon would see the Sun rise—which seems logical enough, except that this direction of east therefore actually appears on the westward or leading edge of the Moon as seen by an observer looking up into Earth's sky!

What follows is a selection of some of the most conspicuous (which by no means includes all of the most remarkable) lunar features. The schedule by which we observe them is day by day in the course of the Moon's progression from one New Moon phase to the next—a *lunation*. The amount of time elapsed since the most recent New Moon is called the Moon's "age." Remember that the exact age at which the terminator reaches lunar features varies somewhat from month to month because of libration. This is yet another reason why you should record your observations with sketches—of the entire crescent at low magnification and of especially interesting regions at high magnification.

Two Days Old. Although the Moon can be observed far "younger" than this age under favorable conditions, even a 2-day-old Moon is often so low that "seeing" (atmospheric steadiness) is likely to be poor. Most experts suggest studying this area near the eastern limb of the Moon just after Full Moon (when the sunset rather than the sunrise terminator is moving across it) because the Moon can then be observed high in the sky for much of the night. In case you still want to look at 2 days old, the outstanding feature is Mare Crisium (Sea of Crises). The *maria* (singular *mare*, Latin for "sea") are the Moon's dark plains of hardened lava. Many can be seen with even the naked eye (they are the dark markings that form "the Man in the Moon" and "the Lady in the Moon"). Mare Crisium is the only major mare on the near side of the Moon that is completely separate from the rest of the maria system—note that it is completely surrounded by bright highlands. Well south of Crisium around this time, the terminator is passing the north–south series of the giant craters Langrenus, Vendelinus, and Petavius. See Figure 3.

Four Days Old. Both Mare Crisium and Mare Fecunditatis are now fully in view, and the Langrenus–Vendelinus–Petavius sequence is well seen. Small but bright Proclus lies just west of Crisium and has Crisium-crossing rays, which under a high Sun are among the most prominent on the Moon. Atlas and Hercules form a superb pair; Atlas is somewhat larger. Note Fracastorius, which was once a crater and now is a "bay" on the edge of Mare Nectaris. Down near the end of the opposite (the south) horn of the crescent are the crater Rheita and the Rheita Valley (not a true valley).

Six Days Old. Now all of Mare Nectaris and Mare Tranquillitatis is lit, as is most of Mare Serenitatis. Aristoteles and Eudoxus are notable neighbors in the highlands between Serenitatis and the east end of Mare Frigoris. Posidonius is prominent on a kind of cape at the east edge of Serenitatis; little Plinius, in the strait between Serenity and Tranquillity.

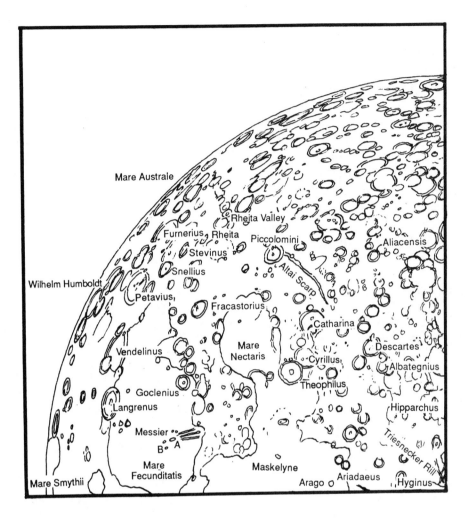

Figure 3 Moon Quadrant 2—Southeast Quadrant. South is up and east is left, as in most telescopes.

Near Plinius is bright Menelaus; similarly small but bright Maskelyne is close to the entrance from Mare Serenitatis to Mare Nectaris. Theophilus, one of the finest craters on the Moon, has walls reaching to 18,000 feet above its floor and a prominent central mass. It overlaps the older, less well-formed Cyrillus and with Cyrillus and Catharina forms a spectacular western border to Mare Nectaris. The Altai Scarp is not far away.

Seven Days Old. Here at First Quarter, we catch many superb craters and mountains near or on the terminator. The Moon's most spectacular mountain range, the Apennines, are partly in view. Within the next day or so, the southwest end of this range will catch sunrise, forming a peninsula of light that even the naked eye can see as a deformation of the terminator. A break between the northeast end of the Apennines and the beginning of the Caucasus Mountains is a strait between Mare Serenitatis and the still mostly dark Mare Imbrium. Just to the Imbrium side of the strait, the craters Aristillus and Autolycus form a fine pair. A little farther north, in the Alps of the Moon, the impressive Alpine Valley now is seen as a prominent cut of shadow through the mountain range. The southern highlands are thick with major craters, and now is the time to see two huge but worn neighbor craters that are difficult to identify near Full Moon—Hipparchus and Albategnius.

Questions

1. Can you ever get a clear view of any features on the Moon when it is less than 2 days old (if so, which are they)? How much of Mare Crisium can you see on the 2-day-old Moon? On the 3-day-old Moon? How does the view vary from week to week and month to month because of libration? How many hours past New Moon does the terminator reach Langrenus, Vendelinus, and Petavius? Can you detect these craters then even in your finderscope?

2. When the Moon is about 4 days old, what are your impressions of Proclus, Atlas and Hercules, Fracastorius, and Rheita and the Rheita Valley?

3. When the Moon is about 6 days old, what are your impressions of Aristoteles, Eudoxus, Posidonius, Plinius, Menelaus, Maskelyne, Theophilus, Cyrillus, and Catharina? Can you get a good view of the central mountain mass of majestic Theophilus? Can you find the Altai Scarp?

4. When the Moon is about 7 days old (near First Quarter), how much of the Apennines can you see? Can you find the Caucasus and Alp Mountains and the Alpine Valley? What are your impressions of Hipparchus and Albategnius? What other craters in the rugged southern highlands can you identify?

3.

Tour of the Moon—Nine- and Ten-Day-Old Moon

Continue our tour from the previous activity by identifying the major surface features of the Moon that the terminator reveals on the key days 9 and 10 of the Moon's lunation. Write down your impressions and sketch the appearance of features such as Copernicus and Eratosthenes, Tycho and Clavius, Ptolemaeus and Alphonsus, the Apennine and Carpathian mountains, Bullialdus and Mare Nubium, Plato, and the many spectacular formations of Mare Imbrium.

In the previous activity, I discussed the system of cardinal directions on the Moon and laid our plan for a day-by-day tour of the Moon's most prominent surface features. Here, we will continue with the second part of this tour.

Nine Days Old. The few days after First Quarter are a busy time for lunar observers. In no other period do so many spectacular features come into view. The terminator is crossing the large extent of Mare Imbrium (Sea of Showers). The southeast rampart of Imbrium is the Apennines, whose whole curving line is now visible. Beyond the southwest end of the Apennines is a superb, well-formed crater, Erastosthenes, and, beyond that, what is generally considered the most magnificent crater on the Moon, Copernicus. As the terminator gets past Copernicus, you can admire the crater's superb form, the great height of its walls, the marvelous central triple-mountain mass, and the remarkable detail in its rough floor. A few days from now, the ring of the crater, its surrounding area, and its rays will glow even brighter. In contrast to the brightness of Copernicus is the dark-floored majesty of Plato, a large crater in the highlands separating Mare Frigoris from Mare Imbrium. On Mare Imbrium itself, though near its northern edge, are the solitary mountains, Pico and Piton, and the line of peaks called the Straight Range—all breathtaking features when their tops catch sunrise above the still shadowed mare floor and later when their shadows lie long across the newly illuminated floor. Archimedes, Aristillus, Autolycus, and Timocharis are prominent craters within Mare Imbrium.

On the 9-day-old Moon, the terminator has already swept past Sinus

11

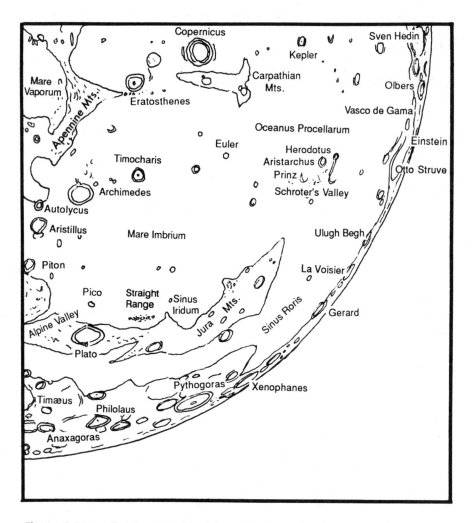

Figure 4 Moon Quadrant 3—Northwest Quadrant. South is up and east is left, as in most telescopes.

Medii (Central Bay), which marks the center of the Moon's face, and past a mighty pair of adjacent ancient craters that sit south of Sinus Medii near the start of the rugged southern highlands—Ptolemaeus and (slightly smaller) Alphonsus. Several other prominent craters that lie near or even abut these are Arzachel, Alpetragius, and Herschel—not to mention Albategnius and fading Hipparchus, which were referred to in our previous activity's notes on the 7-day-old Moon. Farther south are still more great craters near the terminator—among them the famous, young, and

12

beautifully formed Tycho and the foreshortened, old, but enormous Clavius. Most of Mare Nubium is now in view, with the crater Bullialdus very prominent at the sea's northwest edge. Running near Nubium's east edge is the marvelous Straight Wall, a cliff (actually a fault) that now looks like a dark line but that looks dramatically different when it reappears after vanishing for days around Full Moon (see Activity 4).

Ten Days Old. The glorious Sinus Iridum (Bay of Rainbows) is at the terminator. This exquisite cove of Mare Imbrium was perhaps once a dark-floored crater like nearby Plato, only far larger. At this time, the bay's western border, the Jura Mountains, catch the Sun before the lower land and therefore shine out like a "jeweled handle" in darkness. The full length of the Carpathian Mountains, northwest of Copernicus, is now lit, forming a partial boundary between Mare Imbrium and the even vaster, but irregular, "overflow" mare, Oceanus Procellarum (Ocean of Storms). For several days, the great ray-systems of the eastern part of the Moon, those of Proclus and little Stevinus (south of the smaller bright surround of the far larger crater Langrenus), have been prominent. Now the ray-system of Copernicus and the greatest of all, that of Tycho, are glowing ever more prominently.

Questions

1. What are your impressions of Copernicus and Erastosthenes when the Moon is 9 days old? When it is 10 or more days old? How much detail is shown on your sketches of these glorious craters?

2. What are your impressions of the Apennines and the Carpathians when the Moon is 9 and 10 days old? Of Piton, Pico, and the Straight Range during these days?

3. When the Moon is 10 days old, what are your impressions of the entire Mare Imbrium region? Of the Sinus Iridum? Of the craters Archimedes, Aristillus, Autolycus, and Timocharis, which are all on the floor of Imbrium? Of dark-floored Plato, near Imbrium?

4. When the Moon is 8 to 10 days old, what are your impressions of Ptolemaeus and Alphonsus? Of the nearby craters Arzachel, Alpetragius, and Herschel?

5. When the Moon is 9 days old, what are your impressions of Tycho and Clavius? Also of their large neighbor craters? Of Mare Nubium and Bullialdus?

6. When the Moon is about 10 days old, can you trace the ray-systems of Proclus and Stevinus (already brightly lit)? Can you trace some of the rays of Tycho and Copernicus (soon to be magnificent)?

4.

Tour of the Moon—
Twelve-Day-Old, Full, After Full

Continue our tour from the previous two activities by identifying the major surface features of the Moon that the terminator reveals on day 12 of the Moon's lunation, on the day of Full Moon, and on the days after Full Moon. Write down your impressions and sketch the appearance of features such as Kepler, Aristarchus, Herodotus and Schroter's Valley, Mare Humorum and Gassendi, Schiller and Schickard, Bailly, Grimaldi and Riccioli, and Otto Struve. Especially at Full Moon, study the great ray-systems, particularly that of Tycho. After Full Moon, study the sunset terminator's advance, noting any differences between its effect and the sunrise terminator's effect on various features. Around Last Quarter, notice especially the bright appearance of the Straight Wall and the prominence of the ray-system of Byrgius A.

Our day-by-day general tour of the Moon continues . . .

Twelve Days Old. The wonderful, bright companions of Copernicus in Oceanus Procellarum, the craters Kepler and Aristarchus, are now visible. Aristarchus has the greatest surface brightness of any place on the Moon, and both it and Kepler possess superb ray-systems. Very near Aristarchus is contrastingly dark Herodotus, from whose northern wall runs and winds for a long distance the wonderful Schroter's Valley, perceptible even in quite small telescopes. South of Kepler and Oceanus Procellarum, the entire small Mare Humorum is visible, with the huge crater Gassendi on its northern edge. Located down in the southwest part of the Moon, far below Humorum, Schiller is an elongated feature that apparently resulted when the walls separating two craters broke down. Not far away from Schiller, Schickard is a vast, worn crater. But south of Schiller, near the very limb of the Moon, we should now try glimpsing the ancient, worn outline of the largest formation called a crater, or "walled plain," on the near side of the Moon—Bailly, about 180 miles (290 km) across. Even at the most favorable librations, Bailly is so near the southern limb as to be a difficult sight.

Fourteen Days Old—Full Moon. There is little contrast on the

14

Figure 5 Moon Quadrant 4—Southwest Quadrant. South is up and east is left, as in most telescopes.

shadowless Full Moon. This is a time to enjoy the glory of the great ray-systems, especially that of Tycho. The ray that bisects Mare Serenitatis may be derived from Tycho, over a thousand miles away. Now is also the time to get the best look at features near the Moon's western limb. The darkest floor of any crater is that of Grimaldi, which is rivaled by that of nearby (and even more near-the-limb) Riccioli. Down near Schickard is the strange Wargentin, whose inside floor is far higher than the surrounding land outside the crater. Finally, very near the northwest limb, a formation perhaps even larger than Bailly in its north–south dimension can be

15

glimpsed. The catch is that this crater, Otto Struve, seems to be what was originally two craters (as in the case of Schiller).

After Full Moon. As the Moon wanes from Full, rising later and later in our evenings, the sunset terminator on it slides over from lunar east to lunar west, repeating the high-contrast visibility of the first 14 days of features just described. But there are some differences. One of the most beautiful is what happens to the Straight Wall. Appearing as a dark line after First Quarter and disappearing around Full, the Straight Wall then reappears and around Last Quarter is a breathtaking scratch of brilliance as its face, pointing to lunar west, catches full sunlight. Note also on the waning Moon the fading of the previously bright ray-systems. The ray-system that lights up on the waning Moon is that of Byrgius (or, to be accurate, its little companion Byrgius A), located between Mare Humorum and the western limb.

Questions

1. When the Moon is 12 days old, what are your impressions of the great craters Kepler and Aristarchus? Of Herodotus? Can you trace Schroter's Valley running from Herodotus?

2. When the Moon is 12 days old, what are your impressions of Mare Humorum and Gassendi? Of Schiller and Schickard? Can you locate the giant, foreshortened ruin of Bailly?

3. When the Moon is Full, how many ray-systems can you identify? How many rays can you sketch coming from Tycho, and to what distances?

4. When the Moon is Full, what are your impressions of dark-floored Grimaldi and Riccioli? Of strange high-interiored Wargentin? Can you find vast Otto Struve at the western limb?

5. In the days after Full Moon, what are your impressions of the fading ray-systems and the brightening ray-system of Byrgius A? When do you first see the Straight Wall reappear as a bright line, and when is it most prominent?

5.

Selected Craters

Observe all the craters in the following list, sketching each one and its surroundings and trying to note all the details mentioned in the notes below.

In Activities 2 through 4, we took a tour of major lunar features over the course of a lunation. The present activity is to observe—and sketch—in more detail a selection of interesting lunar craters. Remember that the craters chosen represent only a sampling, selected with an eye to offering a variety of detail for the observer. Dozens of other craters hold every bit as much interest for amateur telescopes.

The heights listed below are usually the distance measured from the crater floor up to the crater rim. The abbreviations NE, SE, NW, and SW refer to the northeast, southeast, northwest, and southwest quadrants of the Moon, which are portrayed back in Figures 2, 3, 4, and 5, respectively.

Albategnius. Better preserved than its even bigger neighbor Hipparchus; has central mountain; parts of rim up to over 10,000 feet; SE.

Alpetragius. Terraced walls over 12,000 feet high in places; huge, rounded central mountain mass; SW.

Alphonsus. Smaller than giant neighbor Ptolemaeus, but much detail in floor and has minor central mountain; SW.

Archimedes. Dark floor, with no central mountain; walls average over 4,000 feet with peaks to 7,000 feet; forms a group with Aristillus and Autolycus; NW.

Aristarchus. Brightest crater, but some dark streaks visible with medium-sized telescope; NW.

Aristillus. Close neighbor of slightly smaller and slightly less deep *Autolycus* (both in Mare Imbrium); walls rise to 11,000 feet in places; central mountain mass is triple-peaked; NW.

Aristoteles. Many hills in floor and outside crater; deep; forms bright pair with Eudoxus; NE.

Arzachel. Walls rise to 13,500 feet in places; SW.

Atlas. Much interior detail; terraced walls rise to 11,000 feet; slightly smaller neighbor *Hercules* has walls also to 11,000 feet; NE.

Bailly. Largest crater on near side, but close to south limb; crater walls greatly damaged, but some of the wall peaks up to 14,000 feet; SW.

Bullialdus. Prominently placed; nicely terraced walls up to 8,000 feet; SW.

Clavius. Only slightly smaller than Bailly, but significantly farther from limb; walls up to over 12,000 feet; northeast wall broken by crater Porter; SW.

Cleomedes. Walls average 9,000 feet and are interrupted by 28-mile-wide crater Tralles; NE.

Copernicus. In itself, the Moon's most spectacular crater—"Monarch of the Moon"; walls up to 17,000 feet in places; amazingly complex interior with three central mountain masses and landslide debris extending for many miles inside wall; great brightness and ray-system; NW. See Figure 6.

Endymion. Rather near east limb of Moon; large, with walls to 15,000 feet; NE.

Eratosthenes. One of Moon's most beautifully formed craters; suffers only by comparison to grandeur of neighbor Copernicus; very deep, with central elevations and much detail; NW.

Gassendi. Central mountain, rills (see Activity 7) visible in moderate-sized telescope; breaks in south wall; crater Gassendi A (formerly known as Clarkson) overlaps north wall; SW.

Geminus. Has 16,000-foot walls; central hill; NE.

Grimaldi. Almost as near west limb as neighbor *Riccioli*; both huge, and darkest, craters; SW.

Herodotus. Contrast its darkness with brilliance of nearby Aristarchus; Schroter's Valley begins near its north wall (see Activity 7); NW.

Hipparchus. Nearly as large as Ptolemaeus (just west of Hipparchus), but far more worn; difficult to see except when near terminator; much detail; compare also to neighbor to north, Albategnius; SE.

Kepler. One of brightest and finest craters, with major ray-system intermingling with that of Copernicus at Full Moon; much smaller than Copernicus, but similar in size to its own close neighbor *Encke*—a crater tremendously less prominent and bright than Kepler; superb terracing and central mountain; NW.

Langrenus. Has 9,000-foot terraced walls; twin-peaked central mass; SE.

18

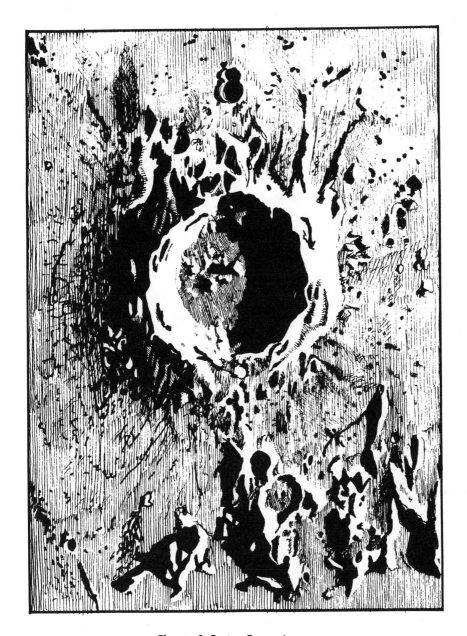

Figure 6 Crater Copernicus.

Macrobius. Walls up to 13,000 feet; compound central mountain; NE.

Maginus. Superb walled plain; overlooked because of even larger neighbor Clavius; SW.

19

Manilius. Brilliant crater at border of Mare Vaporum; terraced walls; central mountain; interior details; NE.

Maskelyne. Rather small but terraced, with central mountain; not far from Apollo 11 landing site; SE.

Menelaus. Fairly small but brilliant crater, with off-center peak inside and walls to 8,000 feet; NE.

Newton. Very near southern limb, but worth trying to observe because it is believed to be the deepest crater on the Moon—the walls rise to more than 20,000 feet above the crater floor; depth and position near pole means some parts of this crater have not been touched with sunlight for billions of years; SW.

Petavius. Greatest of the eastern chain of craters; even more impressive than Langrenus; complex 11,000-foot walls; great central mountain mass and other structure; SE.

Piccolomini. Terraced walls with some peaks up to 15,000 feet; SE.

Plato. Hevelius's "Greater Black Lake"; one of the darkest and (due to its location) one of the most prominent craters on the Moon; NW.

Posidonius. Much detail; craterlet near center; NE.

Proclus. Small but very bright, with rays crossing Mare Crisium and passing to either side of Palus Somnii; 8,000-foot walls; low central mountain; NE.

Ptolemaeus. Giant walled plain near center of Moon's face; slightly larger than more worn neighbor Hipparchus and decidedly larger than less worn neighbor Alphonsus; dark floor; walls up to 9,000 feet in places—but observe when near terminator; SW.

Rømer. Has 11,000-foot walls; large central mountain; NE.

Taruntius. Complete inner wall, like a concentric ring; NE.

Theophilus. Almost as magnificent as Copernicus in structure; 18,000-foot terraced walls; multiple central mountain mass; part of chain with similarly large but much less impressive *Cyrillus* (which it overlaps) and *Catharina*—note highness of region between latter two when whole area is near terminator; SE.

Timocharis. Has 7,000-foot terraced walls; crater at center; NW.

Tycho. Most spectacular crater on Moon when its ray-system is strong near Full Moon; crater itself far less magnificent than Copernicus, but superb with high, terraced walls and great central mountain complex; SW.

Vendelinus. Compare with next giants in chain, Petavius and Langrenus, which are far less worn and more impressive; SE.

Walter. Complex walls; interior mountain off-center; SW.

Wargentin. Crater floor much higher than outside land, as proven by lack of interior shadow—the only very large lunar plateau; SW.

Questions

1. Can you observe all the features of all the craters listed in this activity? What do your sketches and observations reveal about them that is not mentioned here?

2. What other craters or other lunar formations do you notice, identify, and sketch in the course of observing the craters on the list?

6.

Lunar Maria

Observe all the major maria, sketching them, rating their darkness and color, looking for detail on their surfaces, and identifying important craters and other features that are on them or border them.

The maria, or "seas," cover much of the near side of the Moon. The larger ones are big and prominent enough to be easily visible to the naked eye. With a telescope, there is a lot of variety to study in the different maria and learning your way around them is essential if you are going to find most craters and other lunar features.

The following discussion of maria includes mention of a few of the smaller formations—"marshes" and "bays"—which are made of the same dark, hardened lava that flowed when giant bodies impacted the Moon in the early days of the solar system. There is no fundamental difference between a mare ("sea") and a palus ("marsh") or sinus ("bay")—only size. Indeed, only size distinguishes these formations from those of the largest craters, the so-called walled plains, which are dark-floored.

The features are given in approximate order of their appearance during the course of a lunation.

Mare Crisium (Sea of Crises). This rather small mare is conspicuous for several reasons. First of all, it (and it alone of the major seas) is separated from the rest of the maria system. Second, it is not only surrounded entirely by bright highlands, it has also been rated by some observers as the darkest of the maria (some have noted a tinge of green to it, too). Third, Crisium is located on the frequently seen evening crescent, and it is located just far enough from the limb for libration to make very dramatically noticeable changes in its shape and apparent position. The largest crater on Crisium is Picard. The capes on its borders are Cape Livinium, Cape Olivium, and Cape Agarum. Just west of it is the bright crater Proclus, several of whose rays cross Crisium when the Sun gets high.

Palus Somnii (Marsh of Sleep). This little outlier from the Sea of Tranquillity has rays from Proclus passing to either side of it. It is as bright as any of the maria formations (about $3\frac{1}{2}°$ to $4°$ in the $0°$-to-$10°$ scale of brightness, which puts black shadow at $0°$, Grimaldi at $1°$, and Aristarchus at $10°$), a strong contrast to the dark Mare Crisium (which is as dark as $1\frac{1}{2}°$ in places). Palus Somnii is reputed to show a brownish yellow color.

Mare Fecunditatis (Sea of Fertility). The interesting crater Taruntius is in the strait that connects this long sea with Mare Tranquillitatis, and the big three craters of Langrenus, Vendelinus, and Petavius run near its southeast edge. The one large crater within it is Goclenius. The most fascinating craters in it are Messier and Messier A, the latter having twin rays.

Mare Nectaris (Sea of Nectar). This very small mare has the bay of Fracastorius at one end and connects with Tranquillitatis at the other. Near its western border is the superb Theophilus chain. One of Tycho's greatest rays appears to cross Nectaris and go over into Fecunditatis.

Mare Tranquillitatis (Sea of Tranquillity). This sea is connected with four others. British astronomy writer and lunar observer Patrick Moore notes that its floor is lighter and patchier and that its form is less regular than that of its neighbor Serenitatis. Its biggest crater is Plinius, near the strait separating it from Serenitatis. Its greatest distinction (from our point of view) is having been the first place that humans set foot on another world.

Mare Serenitatis (Sea of Serenity). This large and almost circular mare is bounded by major mountain ranges on several sides and has no large craters on it. It has Posidonius at its eastern edge, and little Bessel in its midst is passed by the controversially longest ray from Tycho. Is this ray reinforced at Bessel or at bright Menelaus (a crater on the southern shore of Serenitatis)?

Lacus Somniorum (Lake of the Dreamers). Small outlier of Tranquillitatis. Brightest maria formation along with Palus Somnii. Look for patchiness and some rills on its surface.

Mare Vaporum (Sea of Vapors). Small but dark mare which has the Hyginus Rill system on it, and to which the Ariadaeus Rill runs (see Activity 7).

Sinus Medii (Central Bay). Approximately marks the center of the Moon's earthward face—Earth forever hangs virtually overhead to a viewer in this place. Quite dark.

Mare Nubium (Sea of Clouds). A large and rather ill-defined sea. While some observers think that it is lighter, others think that it is darker than nearby Mare Imbrium. Bullialdus is the one outstanding crater in Mare Nubium, but not far east of it is the great central meridian chain of craters that includes Ptolemaeus, Alphonsus, Arzachel, and others.

Mare Imbrium (Sea of Showers). Usually considered the grandest of the maria, Mare Imbrium is second in size only to Oceanus Procellarum—but Procellarum is an irregular (quite ill-defined) or "overflow" mare, whereas Mare Imbrium is a regular or "impact" mare. The impact that created Imbrium was the most violent event ever in the molding of the Moon's surface. In the next activity, we will deal with the five mountain ranges that form the incomplete boundary of what would otherwise be a full ellipse (the boundary of Imbrium and Procellarum is unmarked on either side of the Carpathian Mountains). We will also look at the mountains on Imbrium itself—the Straight Range, Pico, and Piton. The great craters on Imbrium are Archimedes, Aristillus, Autolycus, and Timocharis. Nearby are dark Plato, bright Aristarchus, magnificent Copernicus, and superb Eratosthenes. And one of the few most beautiful sights on all the Moon is Imbrium's bay, Sinus Iridum.

Sinus Iridum (Bay of Rainbows). This bay off Mare Imbrium was probably once a separate vast crater. Now it is open to Imbrium between Cape Laplace and Cape Heraclides, the latter of which is a "jeweled handle" in darkness when it catches the sunrise before the land below it in the mouth of the bay each month. Cape Heraclides has been pictured as having the shape of a lady facing Imbrium—"the Moon Maiden." From the elevation level of Imbrium, the surface of Sinus Iridum slopes gradually down a full 2,000 feet.

Mare Frigoris (Sea of Cold). This longest and skinniest of the maria extends all the way from near Crisium, past Imbrium and Plato, and at last to join Oceanus Procellarum via Sinus Roris (Bay of Dews). Its color has been described as yellowish green.

Oceanus Procellarum (Ocean of Storms). The largest of the lunar seas, Oceanus Procellarum is bordered on one side by Grimaldi and on the other by Copernicus, and it contains the great craters Kepler and Aristarchus. Its floor is said to be lighter and patchier than that of Imbrium.

Mare Humorum (Sea of Moisture). This round little mare is neighbored by Procellarum and Nubium. At its north border is the giant crater Gassendi; its south and east borders feature the bays Doppelmayer and Hippalus, respectively.

There are many other minor maria and "bays" and "lakes" and "marshes" on the Moon, worth finding for the fun of it. A special project is to look for the maria that are very near the limb during favorable librations (see Activity 9).

Questions

1. Which of the maria are darkest or lightest? What subtle differences in their colors can you notice?
2. Can you sketch all the maria described in this activity at least roughly, and interesting parts of them in detail? What other maria and similar formations do you notice? What new features do you discover for yourself as a result of your study?

7.

Other Lunar Features

Study and sketch our selected mountain ranges and mountains, rills and valleys, faults and domes of the Moon.

The craters of the Moon are myriad and famous; the maria are the markings that the unaided eye has always seen. The other lunar features are far fewer, less conspicuous, and less popularly known. But they are by no means less fascinating. The following information concerns some of the many marvelous mountain ranges and mountains, rills and valleys, and faults and domes of the Moon.

Mountain Ranges and Mountains. The mountain ranges of the Moon are mostly the borders of maria. Mare Imbrium, for instance, has for ramparts the Apennine, Caucasus, Alp, Jura, and Carpathian Mountains. All were presumably thrown up like the walls of an enormous crater when the impact that caused Imbrium occurred (the most violent surface-shaping event in the Moon's history). So the Moon's mountains are much different than Earth's. They do compare favorably in size with all but Earth's tallest ranges, and are far bigger in proportion to the little world on which they are found.

The Apennines are the greatest of the Moon's ranges, extending for 600 miles with peaks up to 18,000 feet high—they form a deformation of the terminator easily noted with the naked eye just after First Quarter. The Alps are best known for being cut by the marvelous Alpine Valley. The Carpathians are not far from majestic Copernicus. Other important ranges around the Moon include the Caucasus, Haemus, and Riphaean.

Isolated mountains on the surface of the maria may form spectacular islands of light, or may cast dramatic long shadows. Pico and Piton are mighty examples in Mare Imbrium. And there is, not far from them in Imbrium, the fine Straight Range—40 miles long, less than 6,000 feet high, but very regular and discrete.

Valleys and Rills. The greatest valley is the Alpine. It splits the Alps for over 80 miles and is a dramatic dark mark in their bright midst around lunar sunrise. Some valleys are really chains of small craters—for instance, the Rheita Valley (this formation is 115 miles long and 15 miles wide, though!). The term *rill* would generally be applied to a cleft narrower than a valley, but the distinctions blur. The most marvelous rill is Schroter's Valley, running out from near Herodotus and twisting dramatically, at one point broadening into what has been called "the Cobra Head." Also superb are the branching rill systems of Hyginus and Ariadaeus, which actually connect to each other, and that of Triesnecker.

Faults and Domes. By far the most notable fault feature on the Moon is the peerless Straight Wall—75 miles long and over 1,000 feet tall with a fairly steep slope (see Activity 4 about its marvelous changes in appearance). Much smaller are the mysterious lunar domes. These small surface swellings can be found in many places on the Moon. Two good areas for finding the domes are near the craters Arago and Prinz.

Questions

1. What is the progression of appearances presented by Pico, Piton, and the Straight Range as the terminator moves across them? Can you identify all the mountain ranges mentioned in this activity? What other ranges can you locate?

2. What do your sketches show of the Alpine Valley, Rheita Valley, and Schroter's Valley? How do these features differ despite the fact that their names suggest they are the same type of formation? How many of the branches of the Hyginus, Ariadaeus, and Triesnecker rill systems can you trace? How much of these systems is visible with telescopes of various sizes?

3. What are your impressions of the Straight Wall on each day of the lunation that it is visible? How does telescope aperture affect its visibility?

4. Can you locate the lunar domes in the areas mentioned here? Can you locate domes in other places (such as in parts of Oceanus Procellarum)?

8.

Lunar Transient Phenomena (LTP)

Look for LTP (lunar transient phenomena) in certain craters and other areas of the Moon that seem to be prone to their occurrence. If you spot what may be an LTP, be sure to sketch the appearance or series of appearances and write down all details about the time, (Earth) atmospheric conditions, telescope used, and other particulars of the observation.

The Moon is not quite a changeless place. Seismometers left there by the Apollo astronauts showed that both meteorite impacts and weak moonquakes do occur. But could any activity on the Moon be producing clouds, obscurations, glows, or flashes visible in Earth-based telescopes?

Apparently so. These LTP, or lunar transient phenomena, have been reported for many decades, but only in recent decades has enough evidence been gathered to establish their reality. Apparently, there is spectroscopic proof of occasional gas emissions from various parts of the Moon, and a correlation has been found between a few of these and LTP sightings. There also seems to be some correlation between the places where moonquakes and LTP have occurred.

The most likely explanation for an LTP is seismic activity in a region leading to gaseous emission that either obscures our view of the surface or is itself visible as an actual cloud—or that actually glows by a strange transformation of the quake's energy into visible light. This process may be the same "triboluminescence" that causes brief glows when certain crystalline candies are impacted (as far back as the mid-1970s, my friends Steve and Becky Vickers showed me the now well-known experiment of crunching a wintergreen Lifesavers candy between your teeth in a dark room to produce brief glows!).

Where are the best places on the Moon to look for LTP? According to studies by Patrick Moore and Barbara Middlehurst and her colleagues (see Moore's *New Guide to the Moon*, pp. 197–212, for a discussion), the areas around the edges of the regular maria, also regions rich in rills, seem to be the most prone to LTP. By far the most common place for them seems to be the brilliant crater Aristarchus. But two other famous craters, Plato and Alphonsus, have also been the scenes of a number of such events. Other craters where LTP have been observed include Grimaldi, Gassendi, Kepler, and Hercules.

What does an LTP look like? In some cases, the phenomenon was detectable only by its reduction of the visibility of lunar surface detail in the isolated region where it occurred (this, for instance, was observed in Plato). Other times, what appeared to be visible mist or cloud filled a crater. Still other times, the event looked merely like a discoloration—usually a reddening—of an area. And then there are the cases of glows and flashes. A 1985 photograph of a flash that seemed to be an LTP was recently proven to have been a glint of sunlight off an Earth-orbiting artificial satellite passing in front of the Moon. But no such explanation will do for another such photograph, taken 4 years before the launch of the first Sputnik!

Now every one of these possible appearances for an LTP can also be produced by far more mundane causes. Defective or dirty optics, conditions in Earth's atmosphere, the tremendous intricacy and changeability of light and shadow in the complex lunar landscape—all of these can give rise to spurious LTP reports. A strong case for an LTP generally can be made only when good sightings of the same alleged event are made by at least two independent observers.

The difficulty of proving an LTP—not to mention the rarity of these phenomena—may discourage many amateur astronomers from deciding to make them the object of any special observing program. Indeed, anyone who is a very devoted and frequent lunar observer stands a reasonable chance of eventually happening upon an LTP anyway. Nevertheless, if you are intrigued by the idea of witnessing these events, and by what we might learn about the nature of the Moon from them, you may wish to make a special effort to see them. Your observing program would then consist of watching the specific craters and the general areas mentioned here with this purpose in mind. Your reward someday might be visible proof that this marvelous Moon is not quite as dead a world as we thought it must be.

Questions

1. Have you ever seen what you think might have been an LTP? What were the circumstances and the full details of the appearance?

2. How much time do you spend watching the supposedly LTP-prone craters? What do you learn about these craters as a by-product of your LTP vigil?

3. What odd changes do you see in lighting or visibility of features from

hour to hour or night to night that are not LTP but that are interesting in their own right?

9.

Libration and Regions Near the Moon's Limb

Take advantage of the most favorable librations to observe features usually too close to the limb to see well or at all. Try to identify as many features that you have not seen before as possible. Take special care to make good sketches of these views—views that might not be repeatable for a long time.

Back in Activity 1, I mentioned in most basic terms what libration was. One of the goals of that activity was to note the effects of libration on some of the major surface features near the Moon's limb. Now it is time to learn how libration works in more detail and to use this knowledge to get better views of elusive maria and craters at the limb.

Libration is a rocking to either side, also up and down, of the face of the Moon pointed toward us. The fact that the Moon takes the same amount of time to rotate as it does to orbit Earth should mean that the Moon always keeps the same face toward us. And it does—but not *exactly* the same face.

There are several causes of the rocking of the Moon, of its not keeping quite exactly the same face toward Earth. Of the several different kinds of libration, only one is due to irregularities in the Moon's rotation. This *physical libration* is a slight wobbling of the Moon as it rotates which occurs because the Moon is not quite a perfect sphere (Earth actually pulls the near side of the Moon to it strongly enough to make this side bulge toward Earth a bit). Physical libration is slight enough to ignore for most observational purposes.

The other kinds of libration all arise purely from changes in our perspective, or vantage-point, on the Moon. Least important is *diurnal libration*. Diurnal libration is caused by the varying viewpoint we have by virtue of being rotated around to different positions by our own world (an observer on Earth at moonrise sees a little farther beyond the Moon's east side, at moonset farther around the Moon's west side). It is largest as seen from Earth's equator but is, in any case, quite slight—and straight-forwardly predictable.

The two kinds of libration that are the largest and that combine together in a rather complex manner are the librations in latitude and longitude.

The *libration in latitude* enables us to see sometimes a bit more of the Moon beyond the Moon's north pole, sometimes a bit more beyond the Moon's south pole. It is caused by the fact that the Moon's axis of rotation is not quite perpendicular to the plane of its orbit.

The *libration in longitude* enables us to see lunar landscape somewhat beyond what we usually can at the Moon's eastern or western limb. It is caused by the fact that the Moon's orbit is not quite circular. When nearer to Earth, the Moon travels faster than its average speed, while its rotation rate stays the same, which enables us to peek a little farther past its trailing edge; when the Moon is farther from Earth, it travels slower than its average speed and we peek past its leading edge.

The librations in latitude and longitude are substantial. The former is over 6½° (that is the tilt of the Moon's axis with respect to its orbit); the latter varies (because the ellipticity of the Moon's orbit varies) but has an average of almost 6½° and a maximum of almost 8°. The catch is that the Moon's attitude toward us at any given time is a combination of both of these librations. Fortunately, in each issue since July of 1987, *Sky & Telescope* magazine has published the results from John Westfall's computer program that takes the selenographic latitude and longitude of Earth and gives one figure for the point on the Moon's limb that is most or least tilted away from us at various times during the current month. This statistic is the most directly useful one for any observer who wants to know how favorable or unfavorable the current libration is for observing various lunar features near the limb.

The most exciting prospect is to find the best time for observing a feature usually too far around the edge to see properly—if at all! Instead of seeing the slightly less than 50 percent of the Moon we would see if it always kept exactly the same face toward us, we can see—at one time or another—up to 59 percent because of libration. This means there is a strip of lunar landscape about 120 miles (about 200 km) wide that is sometimes not visible at all but that at maximum librations comes into at least oblique view.

Table 1 lists lunar maria and craters near the limb that should be observed when a libration is favorable. Remember that you should also consider what the lighting conditions of the features you look for will be (in

Table 1
Selected Features in the Lunar Limb Region

MARIA

Mare Australe	Mare Novum
Mare Humboldtianum	Mare Orientale
Mare Marginis	Mare Smythii

MOUNTAIN RANGES

Cordillera Mountains (outer ring around Mare Orientale)

Rook Mountains (inner ring around Mare Orientale)

(The D'Alembert and Leibnitz mountains are no longer considered true mountain ranges and have been removed from lunar maps.)

CRATERS

Anaxagoras	Neper
Bailly	Newton
Bouvard	Olbers
Einstein	Philolaus
Gauss	Struve, Otto
Gerard	Sven Hedin
Humboldt, Wilhelm	Ulugh Begh
Inghirami	Vasco de Gama
La Voisier	Xenophanes

most cases, the most favorable lighting would be when the terminator is near the area).

By the way, different from the strip we have trouble seeing at all except for libration is the part of the Moon named "Luna Incognita." This area is, it is true, near the south pole of the Moon, but it is actually the area that was never photographed well by any spacecraft. In the 1980s, organizations like ALPO (Association of Lunar and Planetary Observers) encouraged amateur astronomers to study Luna Incognita, with excellent results. Now, in the 1990s, the Galileo spacecraft may get polar views of the Moon that will further improve our coverage. Of course, the fact remains that there will always be fewer observations of Luna Incognita—and of all the limb areas of the Moon—than of the easier, better-placed parts of the Moon's face. So your own observations of these regions can be considered especially valuable.

Above all else, remember to sketch what you see. Conditions for such a view of certain features may not be so favorable (because of libration, lighting angle, sky conditions, and so on), or at least similar, for a long time to come.

Questions

1. What part of the Moon's limb is most favorably librated tonight? What part is least favorably librated? What features that you normally cannot see are visible? How many features that you have never seen before can you identify and sketch?
2. What are the effects of libration on lunar features only moderately close to the limb? Are there any details of them which you find you see better or at least differently than you have seen before?

10.

Lunar Occultations

Observe as many lunar occultations of stars—and certainly any you possibly can of planets—this year. Enjoy the beauty and note the differences of immersion and emersion at various parts of the Moon's bright limb and its dark limb. Watch for a two-step event if the star being occulted is known to be a double star (or even if it is not already known to be a double star). Observe as many grazing occultations as you can drive to and consider perfecting your timing technique well enough to submit accurate results to IOTA.

The previous activity was concerned with observing the limb regions of the Moon. But there is a special way that amateur astronomers can learn precise information about the topography of these regions that does not even involve observing them directly. The way to do it is to observe a kind of event that is truly spectacular in its own right—a lunar occultation.

To "occult" means to hide; so an *occultation* is the hiding of one celestial body by another. The Moon can sometimes occult a planet—an event of especially great interest—but more common are lunar occultations of stars.

A lunar occultation will be visible only if the star is bright enough to be seen in close proximity to the Moon. The larger your telescope, the fainter the star you can see, but there are other variables. The phase of the Moon is an obvious one. Even the occultation of a naked-eye star will be difficult to see well if it involves the Full Moon. Equally important is whether the event being observed is at the bright (sunlit) limb or dark limb of the Moon and whether the event is an immersion (disappearance behind the Moon's limb) or emersion (reappearance from behind the Moon's limb). If you read the predicted time of a star's emersion, you should also find out at what limb angle (0° for north, 90° for east, and so on) the emersion will occur. Even so, you may find that you miss the instant that the star winks back into view.

Where do you find out the details about upcoming occultations? Although the popular astronomy magazines generally have information on important occultations (especially in the articles on the coming year's prospects in the January issues), the best source is IOTA, the International Occultation Timing Association (see the "Sources of Information" section). And, as you can gather from this organization's name, the way to contribute to science through observing occultations is by timing them.

One discovery that is possible during occultations is that the star being occulted is actually a very close "double star"—that is, not the single point of light it seems to be, but actually two stars appearing extremely near each other in the sky (often because they really are going through space together as a true pair). If you accurately time the immersion or emersion of a single star, you will find that it is virtually instantaneous. But a double star's light will disappear in two stages—with the time between disappearances telling us the separation of the pair.

More often, occultations are used to tell us about the lunar limb—and this can be done tremendously well in the case of a *grazing occultation*. A "graze" occurs when the Moon's limb so nearly misses the star that you see the star creeping along the limb, only occasionally winking out of view (sometimes only partly out of view—dimming just a bit). When the star disappears or fades, it is passing briefly behind a mountain or highland on the edge of the Moon. In short, timing when a star winks off and on (or dims and brightens) can provide extremely precise information about the altitude of topography at the lunar limb.

If all of this sounds too good to be true, you are right. Timing lunar occultations can be grueling work, requiring both skill and stamina. Other requirements are a good telescope and, often, a good car. The zone on Earth's surface from which a grazing occultation occurs is long but only as wide as the variation in lunar topography involved—thus a few miles wide at most. So you will have to drive a considerable distance if you hope to see several fairly good grazing occultations a year (a regular occultation will normally be viewable over a rather large area of Earth).

A crucial requirement for timing a grazing occultation is of course an accurate means of timing. One means of timing that can give the fraction-of-a-second precision needed is to tape-record the time signals provided (in North America) by the shortwave radio station WWV in the background while the observer presses a buzzer or taps the microphone or utters quick words (like "in" for star hidden and "out" for star revealed). Afterward, the tape is played back and timed with a stopwatch, and the observer's reaction time is subtracted. Note that there are commercially available radios for less than $50 that pick up WWV. But in case you think you can record the events in an easier way and still be accurate, or if you have any questions about the occultation timing procedure, you should write to IOTA. Indeed, you will want to practice on several easier events and review your IOTA information carefully before taking on the challenge of this task seriously for science.

Of course, you can be a less scientifically rigorous observer of occultations, too. There are few sights in astronomy more breathtaking than seeing a glittering point of light teetering on the brink and then almost seeming to be sucked behind the body of that exquisite Moon. Or, likewise, of the star suddenly bursting out from behind an invisibly dark part of the Moon as if it were being created and shining for the first time.

Questions

1. How many lunar occultations of stars can you see this year? Can you see any of planets? What are your impressions of these events? Do you detect a two-step disappearance or reappearance (immersion or emersion) when the object occulted is a double star?

2. Can you drive to, and witness, any grazing occultations this year? How many disappearances or fadings do you see during a particular graze? Do you succeed in doing accurate timing and mailing your results to IOTA?

11.

Manned and Unmanned Spacecraft Landing Sites on the Moon

Locate as many as possible of the sites where manned and unmanned spacecraft have landed on the Moon. Observe and sketch these areas while reviewing the facts about the missions and pondering their significance.

We live in a time of space exploration whose revelations are in many respects even greater than those that followed the first astronomical uses of the telescope. Each one of us should feel like a Galileo. To restore this feeling—or perhaps gain it for the first time—an excellent pursuit is to locate and observe the places on the Moon where human beings and their machines have landed. Indeed, these grand achievements are in dire need of being restored to the memory of society in general—along with the Moon they gave tantalizing looks and information about.

The map in Figure 7 shows the approximate positions of all the manned landing sites and several of the most important unmanned ones. What follows here are notes about them and about other landings. The dates are the time of launch, unless otherwise noted. The longitudes are measured east or west from the Moon's central meridian, which passes through Sinus Medii. The Ranger, Surveyor, and Apollo spacecraft were U.S. ventures; the Luna and Lunokhod spacecraft were Soviet.

> *Luna 2.* Arrived at Moon September 12, 1959. First probe to reach lunar surface. Four weeks later, Luna 3 obtained first photos of Moon's far side.
>
> *Ranger 7.* Arrived at Moon July 31, 1964. Obtained first close-up photos before crashing.
>
> *Ranger 8.* February 17, 1965. Similar to Ranger 7. Crashed in Mare Tranquillitatis.
>
> *Ranger 9.* March 21, 1965. Similar to Rangers 7 and 8. Crashed in western Oceanus Procellarum.
>
> *Luna 9.* Arrived at Moon February 3, 1966. First to soft-land and take photographs of lunar surface.

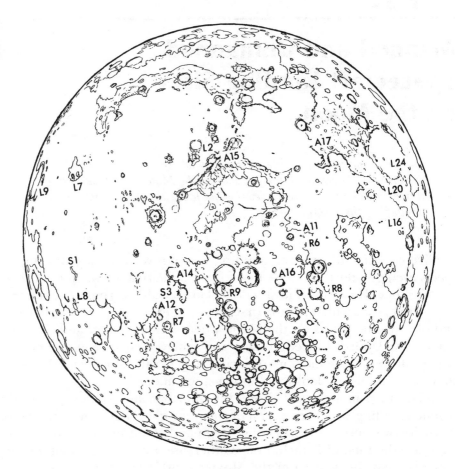

Figure 7 Spacecraft Landing Sites on the Moon. Abbreviations: A—Apollo; L—Luna or Lunokhod; R—Ranger; S—Surveyor.

Surveyor 1. May 30, 1966. Soft-landed and took photos north of Flamsteed.

Luna 13. December 21, 1966. Soft-landed and took photos in western Oceanus Procellarum.

Surveyor 3. April 17, 1967. Soft-landed in Oceanus Procellarum at what eventually became Apollo 12 site. Took photographs and performed first soil experiments.

Surveyor 5. September 8, 1967. Similar to Surveyor 3, but landed in Mare Tranquillitatis about 15½ miles from what eventually became the Apollo 11 site.

Surveyor 6. November 7, 1967. Similar to Surveyors 3 and 5, but landed in Sinus Medii.

Surveyor 7. January 17, 1968. Similar to Surveyors 3, 5, and 6, but landed at north rim of Tycho.

Luna 15. July 13, 1969. Unsuccessful attempt to bring back a lunar sample with an unmanned spacecraft. Location: Mare Crisium.

Apollo 11. Arrived July 20, 1969. First landing of human beings on Moon—Armstrong and Aldrin, with Collins orbiting above in command module. "Tranquility Base" location: latitude 0°67′N, longitude 23°49′E, in Mare Tranquillitatis. (For detailed discussion and charts to help telescopic observers find as closely as possible where the site is, see July 1989 *Sky & Telescope*, p. 84.)

Apollo 12. Arrived November 19, 1969. Astronauts Conrad, Bean, and Gordon. Landed in Oceanus Procellarum at latitude 3°12′S, longitude 23°23′W. Conrad and Bean traversed 0.8 mile outside their lunar module, including a visit to Surveyor 3 (see page 36)!

Luna 16. September 1970. Successful automatic soil return mission. Landed in Mare Fecunditatis at latitude 0°41′S, longitude 56°33′E.

Lunokhod 1. November 1970. First automatic "crawler." Traveled about 12½ miles in western Oceanus Procellarum.

Apollo 14. Arrived February 5, 1971. Astronauts Shepard, Mitchell, and Roosa. Landed at Fra Mauro at latitude 3°40′S, longitude 17°28′E. EVA (extravehicular activity) of 2.1 miles.

Apollo 15. Arrived July 30, 1971. Astronauts Scott, Irwin, and Worden. Landed beside Hadley Rill and the Apennines at latitude 26°6′N, longitude 3°39′E. EVA of 17 miles.

Luna 20. February 1972. Successful automatic soil return mission. Landed in Apollonius region at latitude 3°32′N, longitude 56°33′E.

Apollo 16. Arrived April 21, 1972. Astronauts Young, Duke, and Mattingly. Landed at Descartes at latitude 8°59′S, longitude 15° 31′E. EVA of 16 miles.

Apollo 17. Arrived December 11, 1972. Astronauts Cernan, Schmitt, and Evans. Landed at Taurus–Littrow at latitude 20°10′N, longitude 30°46′E. EVA totaled a record distance of 18 miles and record duration of 22 hours.

Lunokhod 2. January 1973. Automatic "crawler." Traveled about 19 miles in vicinity of Le Monnier.

Luna 24. August 1976. Successful automatic soil return mission. Landed in southeastern Mare Crisium, about midway between craters Picard and Condorcet. The last spacecraft to date (1991) to land on Moon.

Questions

1. How many of the manned and unmanned landing sites can you observe? What are the smallest lunar features you can behold in the vicinity of the manned landing sites?

2. What facts about the various missions to the Moon can you research and read about? What aspects of the missions most intrigue you? What are your thoughts as you observe and sketch these places where humanity has touched the Moon?

12.

General Observations of the Sun

If you do not already know them, learn the basic procedures and safety precautions involved with projecting the Sun's image with a telescope. Sketch the appearance and positions of sunspots. Note the limb darkening of the Sun. Look for faculae, especially near the limb, and try to see which, if any, sunspot group they are associated with today or in the days ahead.

The Sun is the central body of our solar system, the ultimate power source behind virtually all that is active and certainly all that is living on our world. The Sun is also the one outstanding close example of what is so integral a unit of the cosmos as to be visible by the millions in even a small telescope—a star. Sometimes, you have to wonder why a majority of astronomy is not simply devoted to the study of the Sun.

One reason many casual skywatchers or even fairly advanced amateur astronomers do not observe the Sun, however, is the need for either special equipment or special techniques. The Sun is, after all, the only celestial object that is actually dangerous to observe improperly: A moment's mistaken glance at its direct brilliance through a telescope can be enough to blind you permanently.

The peril of the Sun's blinding brightness must never be forgotten, and it is true that some of the special equipment for observing it safely does cost quite a bit of money. The solution for most observers who want to view the Sun safely and inexpensively is an easy technique for which the only "equipment" needed is a screen of some kind (even a piece of cardboard will do). This technique (if performed properly) is safer than using a solar filter (which could conceivably crack) because it does not involve looking at the Sun directly. The technique is known as *projection*.

Projection can be done by letting the Sun shine through a pinhole in a piece of cardboard (onto another piece of cardboard used for a screen) —or even through the chinks between leaves of shade trees! But in order to see the details of features on the Sun, magnification needs to be used— and thus the projection has to be from the eyepiece of a telescope.

How do you get the Sun to shine into the narrow field of your telescope if you cannot search to get it in looking through the eyepiece? Simply move your telescope around until its tube casts the smallest possible shadow on the ground. When the telescope shadow is smallest, the Sun ought to be shining into the telescope, through the eyepiece, and out onto whatever kind of screen you want to set up. Without ever even facing the direction of the Sun, you have brought an image of it onto a screen for your safe perusal.

For a quick look, you can hold a piece of white cardboard out beyond the eyepiece, but obviously a fixed screen (attached to the telescope or standing separately) is needed if you want to keep your image and focus steady. Whatever your setup, having your screen in shadow (shielded from the sunlight coming directly from the sky) is advisable for producing an image with better contrast.

To get your projected image sharp, you merely adjust your focusing knob. But you will find that for each screen distance there is a different focus and that the image is of a different size and brightness. The farther away the screen is, the larger the image of the Sun. But the brightness of the image decreases with distance (proportional to the square of the distance). The observer should therefore find the best compromise: The screen should ideally be at the distance where you have a large enough image of the Sun to see small solar features well but a bright enough image for the features not to suffer from lack of contrast.

Before we discuss what you will see when you get your good projected image of the Sun, a few more important points should be noted about the dangers of solar viewing.

I do not recommend that any novice observer try using solar filters. In fact, I feel that even more experienced amateur astronomers should only do so after having a direct and thorough demonstration of the filters' use by someone who is already a veteran. The image obtained with a high-quality filter is a little bit better than that obtained by projection. But, frankly, many amateur astronomers may find that this slight advantage is not worth the added expense, trouble, and risk.

If full sunlight is being focused by your telescope, there are certain places where the heat will be very great. The image of the Sun on your screen fans out from a point beyond the eyepiece (actually the exit pupil) where so much heat is concentrated that paper there can easily be burned. But, since within the eyepiece there is also considerable heat, any eyepiece with cemented lenses stands the danger of having the cement melt and the eyepiece be ruined. Do not risk an expensive ocular on solar observing!

Not only certain kinds of eyepieces, but also certain kinds of telescopes, are inadvisable to use on the Sun. Unless you use a suitable full-aperture or off-axis filter, solar observing should not be attempted with a Schmidt–Cassegrain or any other telescope that has a closed tube and compound optics because the buildup of heat could certainly melt cements in the optical system. Neither is it advisable to use a telescope of large aperture. As you get apertures larger than about 6 inches, the heat problem becomes more severe and you are rarely, if ever, compensated with a better image because of the bad "seeing" caused by daytime heating. Note that it is advisable to turn even a small telescope off the Sun about every 10 minutes to allow some cooling. Also, a grassy field is one of the best sites for minimizing the local heating effects that contribute to bad "seeing."

As you can see, solar observing does require some special precautions and special techniques. But the payoff is great. When you look at your projected image of the Sun, you are snatching a safe and clear vision from out of what is otherwise that elemental blinding patch in the sky. What do you see?

Almost always, even a very small telescope should show the famous sunspots. See Figure 8. Day after day, they are changing, some appearing and others disappearing, many altering their form, all moving across the face of the Sun because of the Sun's rotation. They have structure and come singly or in pairs or groups. Their numbers increase and decrease rather unpredictably over the short term, but far more predictably over the course of the 11-year cycle of solar activity. Speaking of activity, our next two activities are all about sunspots.

But there are a few other features you can see in the projected image of the Sun fairly easily. One is the *limb darkening*. The edge of the Sun appears less bright, almost dusky in comparison to the middle. Limb darkening is caused by the absorption of light by gases above the blindingly bright visible surface of the Sun, the *photosphere*. Near the edge of the Sun, we are looking grazingly through a greater thickness of the gases, and the photo-

Figure 8 View of Sunspots Near the Sun's Limb.

sphere is accordingly fainter. You can also see another feature, the bright areas called *faculae*. These are bright clouds of hydrogen floating above the photosphere (or in the "upper photosphere"). They are usually only bright enough to appear brighter than the photosphere (and hence be noticeable) when they are near the darkened limb. Faculae may appear in an area where a sunspot group is about to form, and they may continue to be visible for a long time after the sunspot group fades. They should not be confused with solar flares, brief brilliant outbursts that are rarely visible without special filters—only if you are lucky may you someday see for a matter of minutes a bright white-light flare.

Questions

1. With each telescope and eyepiece combination you use, what seems to be the optimum screen distance for getting the best combination of Sun image size and brightness?

41

2. What is the number and the appearance of the sunspots that you see and sketch? Do you notice the limb darkening? Are any faculae visible, and, if so, do they appear to be associated with any sunspot group then or soon after?

13.

Structure of Sunspots and Sunspot Groups

Study and sketch the structure of sunspots carefully, noting any penumbra that may surround the umbra of a spot. Look for and draw spot pairs and spot groups. When "seeing" conditions are unusually good, sketch sunspots at the start and end of an hour to see whether you can identify any changes even in so short a time.

What is a sunspot? We know that it is a cooler, dimmer region of the Sun's photosphere—but only relatively cooler and dimmer (the temperature is still thousands of degrees, and a direct, unfiltered view of a sunspot would still be blinding). The cause of this reduction in brightness and heat is a cutting off of energy from the Sun's lower levels that is caused by a powerful magnetic current. The sunspot is the surface manifestation of what is thought to be a kind of magnetic vortex below the surface.

Actually, the magnetic field is thought to usually come up out of the photosphere at one point, where a sunspot or sunspots appear, and arc to return into the photosphere at another point, where another sunspot or several other sunspots appear. Not always is the second associated spot (or spots) visible (for one thing, it forms after the first). Seldom does the observer see one simple spot clearly paired with another simple spot. But many of the sunspot groups show some degree of symmetry in their pattern, and this is the indication that we are seeing sunspots at the associated magnetic exit and magnetic reentrance points—a *bipolar sunspot group*.

Of course, the simplest aspect of sunspot structure is the distinction between the darker, cooler central area, or *umbra*, of a spot and the less dark, not as cool surrounding region, or *penumbra*. Some spots seem to be all umbra; others display penumbra.

Figure 9 shows examples of the different major classifications of sunspots made on the basis of their structure or structure of their group. A description of each class follows:

A. Small spot or small spot group with no penumbra.

B. Small group of spots with no penumbra but exhibiting association with one another, or symmetrical patterning (bipolar group).

C. Bipolar group with largest members surrounded by one penumbra.

D. Bipolar group in which major spots have a penumbra.

E. Very large bipolar group (larger than 10° across) in which major spots exhibit a complex penumbra and most (or all) minor spots have a penumbra.

F. Largest bipolar groups (15° or larger) surrounded by complex penumbra but still showing some random small spots.

G. Largest bipolar groups (15° or larger) surrounded by complex penumbra but with no random spots.

H. Large spot (larger than 2½°) surrounded by a penumbra, with random small spots nearby.

J. Single spot with a penumbra.

Some groups are difficult to classify because they appear to be truly irregular. Furthermore, any group near the Sun's limb is foreshortened enough to make classification tricky at best. But this raises the interesting matter of the Sun's rotation and of the duration and life cycle of sunspots.

Like all celestial bodies we know, the Sun does rotate. But since the Sun's surface is not a solid, the rotation rate differs for different latitudes, with the equator being the fastest. How fast? A sunspot at the Sun's equator would take about 26.7 Earth-days to make one complete trip around the Sun (if this seems like a slow rotation, consider that a journey around the Sun's equator is well over 100 times longer than a journey around Earth's equator). At a solar latitude of 40°, the rotation is about 29 days; at a solar latitude of 60°, about 31 days. (In the next activity, we will discuss the manner in which sunspots appear at certain latitudes during certain parts of the 11-year cycle of solar activity.)

The average time from a first sunspot's appearance until the fullest development of that spot's group is roughly 10 days (many groups endure far more briefly). Thus, much of a typical group's life may be followed during the course of its passage across the hemisphere of the Sun facing us.

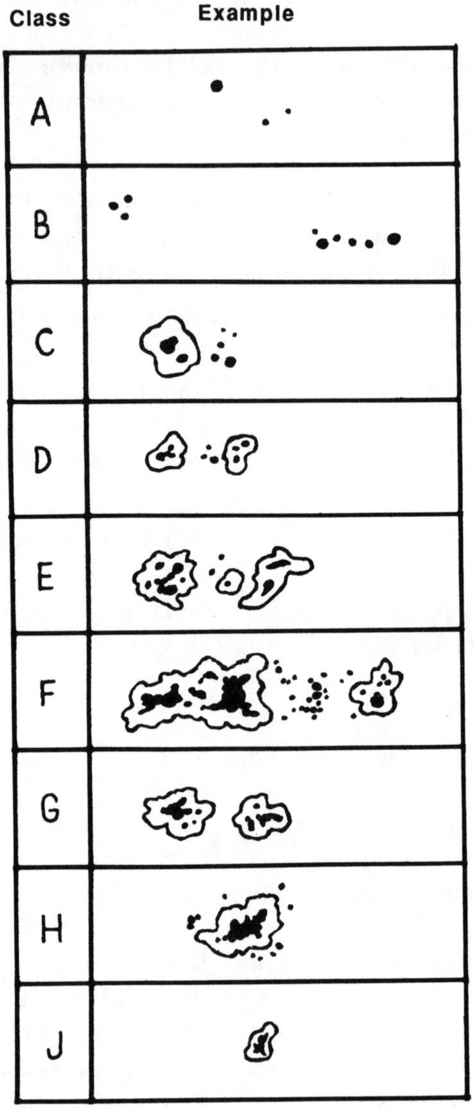

Class   Example

Figure 9 Sunspot Classifications. (See text for description of classes.)

We are very fortunate to see a group survive long enough to reappear at the limb for a second trip across the solar face. But the same area may at least stay unsettled and active, prone to another group's formation.

On the other hand, sunspots may change rapidly enough for the differences to be noticed in just an hour or two. On a day of unusually good "seeing," try observing and sketching a spot or group at intervals about an hour apart to see whether you can detect any change.

The life and circumsolar journey of sunspot groups is absolutely fascinating to follow. And doing so with careful sketches and classification can make the experience far more rewarding.

Questions

1. How many of the sunspots and sunspot groups that you see include a penumbra? What changes in a spot or group, if any, can you detect by making detailed sketches a mere hour apart?

2. Which groups that you observe seem to evidence a symmetry in the pattern of their spots that suggests they are bipolar groups? To which specific class does each group or spot belong?

3. How much of a group or spot's life can you follow as it is carried across the Sun's face by the solar rotation? Can you ever see the same group survive to reappear for a second passage across the face? Can you confirm that new spots have appeared in the same active region that produced other spots on its last trip across the face?

14.

Sunspot Counts

Count all the sunspots and sunspot groups you can see on the Sun each day and do the simple calculation to come up with your Relative Sunspot Number (RSN). Compare your RSNs with those of the official organizations observing the Sun and thereby determine what your personal correction factor should be to standardize your results. Note the change over months in the numbers of sunspots due to the 11-year cycle of solar activity.

Part of our previous activity was the sometimes difficult task of identifying the class to which each sunspot or sunspot group belonged. You might think that counting sunspots would be a far easier project, thus deserving to be an earlier activity. In reality, to tally the special *Relative Sunspot Num-*

ber (RSN) requires some understanding of what constitutes a sunspot group—hence the need for the previous activity to come first.

The RSN is obtained by taking the number of sunspot groups, multiplying this number by 10, and then adding to that amount the number of individual sunspots. The formula is: $RSN = (g \times 10) + n$, where g is the number of sunspot groups and n is the number of individual sunspots.

Let's take an example. Suppose you look at your projected image of the Sun and see two sunspot groups, one composed of 3 sunspots and the other composed of 6 sunspots. The total number of groups (g) is 2. We multiply this by 10 and obtain 20. The total number of spots (n) is 9. We add this to 20 and get as our final total a Relative Sunspot Number (RSN) of 29.

One very important detail to mention is that for RSN purposes even a solitary spot that is not a member of a group must be counted both as an individual spot and as a group. Thus, if there were a group of 3 spots and also a solitary single spot on the Sun, you would consider this as 4 individual spots and (for RSN purposes) as 2 groups. The formula would then be filled in as $(2 \times 10) + 4$, which is $20 + 4$, or 24 for the RSN.

You can see that the RSN is weighted to give additional importance to the existence of groups (the multiplying by 10) and to the presence of any separate outbreak of a spot or spots (thus even individual spots get counted twice—once as a spot, once as a "group"). This is an attempt to provide a better measure of the extent and degree of solar activity than a mere tally of spots could.

There is one further step in obtaining a really useful RSN—multiplying the number you obtain by a value that represents your personal factor as an observer of a certain ability with a certain telescope. In other words, it is important to standardize the counts. The standard can be the daily results of the AAVSO Solar Division or those of the Sunspot Index Data Center in Brussels, Belgium, both of which are reported in each issue of *Sky & Telescope*. (You will have to wait awhile, though, because a given issue presents the results of four months earlier. However, a weekly mean sunspot from two experts is given in most weeks' updated *Sky & Telescope* "Skyline" phone message—see the "Sources of Information" section.)

So, how do you bring your own RSN into accord with that of one of the official sources? You simply determine what your personal correction factor (k) is. This k is simply the number that, when multiplied by your RSN, will give the official RSN. If your telescope is rather large and your eyesight sharp, you may find that you typically get a higher RSN than the official sources. In this case, you would have to multiply by a number less than 1. On the other hand, if the AAVSO number is 99 and yours is 66, then the correction factor (for that day at least) would be 1.5 since $1.5 \times 66 = 99$.

Eventually, you obtain an average difference between your RSNs and those of the official source and figure our your *k*. To determine it can be important. Suppose, for instance, that you are one of the few careful observers of the Sun in your part of the world who actually gets a chance to obtain a good RSN during a time of widespread bad weather. What should the expert make of your figure? If you have figured out your *k* from many previous observations, the answer will be clear and your information valuable.

After many months of doing sunspot counts, you should notice a clear trend in the numbers—either an increase or a decrease. You are witnessing the development of the fascinating 11-year cycle of solar activity. Actually, the time from one solar maximum (maximum numbers of sunspots) and the next only *averages* about 11 years, tending to be a shorter period when there is a rise to an especially powerful maximum. The fall from maximum to minimum is usually slower than the rise back to maximum that follows.

Another intriguing manifestation of the solar cycle is the change in the solar latitudes at which sunspots are seen. At minimum, as a new cycle begins, sunspots begin appearing at middle latitudes of the Sun (seldom more than 40° north or south of the solar equator). As the cycle progresses, the spots show up ever nearer to the Sun's equator. Sunspots rarely appear within 5° of latitude of the solar equator. But, as the old cycle ends and a new one begins, it is sometimes possible to see the last spots of the old cycle near the equator and the first of the new at a middle latitude.

Questions

1. How many sunspots can you count on the Sun today? How many sunspot groups? What is the Relative Sunspot Number (RSN) that you obtain from this observation? How does it compare with the RSN of one of the expert solar organizations? After many such comparisons of observations, what do you figure your personal correction factor *k* to be?
2. How rapid is the increase or decrease of sunspot numbers due to the solar cycle this year? At what solar latitudes are spots currently appearing?

15.

General Observations of Partial Solar Eclipses

Project the image of the Sun onto a screen with your telescope (taking all necessary safety precautions) and observe the progress of the Moon's silhouette across this image. Note the times when you first and last see the Moon and how these compare with the predictions for your site. Determine how large the "magnitude" is and when it occurs for your location by safely measuring the size of the Sun and Moon images at different stages of the eclipse.

It is a disappearing act that is otherwise difficult to share with many people at once. But if you project the image of the Sun from your telescope onto a screen during a partial solar eclipse, as large a crowd as you wish to gather can enjoy the show together. See Figure 10.

The basic techniques and statistics you need to know for solar projection are given back in Activity 12. Even in ordinary solar projection, there is a special eerie thrill you feel in drawing from out of the blinding radiance in the sky a sharp, "live" picture of the Sun and some of its major features. But in observing a partial solar eclipse this way, an even greater feeling of magic is experienced: Here, the fact that the view is "live" is proven spectacularly by the actual progression of the Moon's silhouette across the image.

In suspense, you wait for the moment the Moon's edge first breaks the circle of the Sun and find out how near to the predicted time you can first detect the tiny black indentation. Harder to gauge for an observer is the exact time of maximum eclipse and the *magnitude* (in this case, not "magnitude" in the sense of brightness, but the maximum percentage of the Sun's diameter that gets hidden by the Moon). Why not just measure the Sun and Moon with a ruler on your screen every few minutes? (Careful—remember never to let the beam of light hit your eyes and remember to avoid putting your hand at the point where your eyepiece focuses the most heat!) Naturally, you will want to follow the hypnotizing progress of the Moon after maximum eclipse until the last piece of it moves off the Sun and to note that time.

Where do you learn what time these events will occur and exactly how great the magnitude will be, as seen from your location during an eclipse? The astronomy magazines and good almanacs (especially the "offi-

Figure 10 Partially Eclipsed Sun.

cial" source, the *Astronomical Almanac*) can help. They give the magnitudes and times at a number of cities but generally also tell you how to interpolate (sometimes on a map with eclipse magnitude and time grid lines) to find the correct figures for your site if it is not one of these cities.

Even if there was nothing more to observing a partial solar eclipse by projection than this, there would be little danger of getting bored at any one eclipse or after seeing several. Table 2 lists all strictly partial solar eclipses visible between 1991 and 2003. (A look at Table 3 in our next activity shows total and annular eclipses, which are also partial over large areas of the world surrounding their paths of "totality" and "annularity" and which in these paths are partial before and after the central event of totality or annularity.) But if you add up the number of chances to see a partial solar eclipse in one

Table 2
Partial Solar Eclipses, 1990–2003*

Date	Time§	Maximum Magnitude**
1992 Dec 24	1	0.84
1993 May 21	14	0.74
1993 Nov 13	22	0.93
1996 Apr 17	23	0.88
1996 Oct 12	14	0.76
1997 Sep 2	0	0.90
2000 Feb 5	13	0.58
2000 Jul 1	20	0.48
2000 Jul 31	2	0.60
2000 Dec 25	18	0.72

(No partial-only solar eclipses in 1990–91 or 2001–03)

* Data derived from Jean Meeus, *Astronomical Tables of the Sun, Moon, and Planets.* Listing is of partial-only solar eclipses. For total and annular solar eclipses, which have partial phases, see Table 3.

§ Time of mideclipse, given in hours of Universal Time (see "Note on the Measurement of Time, Position, Angular Distance, and Brightness in Astronomy"). If this time falls within the daylight hours at your location, there is a fair chance you will see at least a small partial eclipse.

** Maximum "magnitude"—not brightness here, but the fraction of the Sun's diameter covered by the Moon.

way or another at any given location, you will find the number to be rather small even in the course of an entire lifetime. And Tables 2 and 3 only begin to suggest how different—in magnitude, in place of visibility, in time of year, and in the Moon's path across the Sun—all these eclipses are.

Questions

1. When do you first and last see any of the Moon in front of the Sun in your projected image during the eclipse? How do these times compare with those predicted for your location?

2. When do you measure (with a ruler) the greatest percentage of the Sun's diameter being covered, and what is this percentage? How do these figures compare with the predicted values?

16.

Observations of Total Solar Eclipses

Study the solar corona during a total eclipse of the Sun, noting structures in the inner, middle, and outer coronas, as well as the angular distances to which each extends. Look for solar prominences of different types during totality.

A total eclipse of the Sun is generally considered the most awesome sight in all of astronomy and is perhaps the most awesome natural event that occurs regularly and can be predicted. Even the most confirmed of telescope users will be lured away from the eyepiece to behold naked-eye wonders of the sky and landscape and the flower of the corona-bordered black Moon blooming in that overall scene of ineffable majesty. Indeed, not just the naked eye, but all the senses—even touch (as the eclipse wind blows) and temperature-sense (as the temperature plummets)—come into play.

Having said all this, however, is not to deny that the central sight of the event—the eclipsed Sun—is seen in its greatest and most fascinating details through the telescope. And, from Table 3, considering how rarely total solar eclipses occur at places easily accessible to the average person's travel budget (let alone to a person staying in one location for all of his or her life), you will want to make the most of this rare and brief telescopic opportunity.

Without special filters or other equipment, the view of the partial phases will need to be by projection. Note that the annular eclipses listed in Table 3 are basically like very large partial solar eclipses in that you will be able to see them only by projection (or with filters), although the climax will be the strange "annulus" or ring of photosphere around the smaller silhouetted form of the slightly too-distant Moon.

Even a mere moment before totality, the direct telescopic view should not be attempted. The breathtaking *Baily's beads* and *diamond-ring effect* observed as totality is starting or ending are dangerously bright to be observed directly with any optical aid. Even a binocular view of the last instant of a "diamond" at the start of totality or the last moments of the *chromosphere's* visibility at the start of totality may be gambles if you do not know exactly what you are doing—and gambling with your eyesight is a perilous game.

51

Table 3
Total and Annular Solar Eclipses, 1991–1996*

Date	Time§	Max. Dur.**	Type	Area of Visibility§§
1991 Jan 15	24	7m, 55s	Annular	S.W. Australia, Tasmania, New Zealand, Pacific
1991 Jul 11	19	6m, 54s	Total	Pacific, Hawaii, Mexico, Central and S. America
1992 Jan 4	23	11m, 42s	Annular	Pacific
1992 Jun 30	12	5m, 20s	Total	Atlantic
1994 May 10	17	6m, 14s	Annular	E. Pacific, N. America, Atlantic, N.W. Africa
1994 Nov 3	14	4m, 24s	Total	S. America, S. Atlantic
1995 Apr 29	18	6m, 38s	Annular	Pacific, S. America
1995 Oct 24	5	2m, 10s	Total	Asia, Borneo, Pacific

(No total or annular solar eclipses in 1996)

* Data derived from Jean Meeus, *Astronomical Tables of the Sun, Moon, and Planets.* Note that all these eclipses also have partial phases and large regions around the path of totality or annularity in which a partial-only eclipse is seen.

§ Time of mideclipse, given in hours of Universal Time (see "Note on the Measurement of Time, Position, Angular Distance, and Brightness in Astronomy").

** Maximum duration, in minutes and seconds, of the total or annular part of the eclipse.

§§ Of the total or annular part of the eclipse.

The time to really begin observations with an unfiltered telescope is once total eclipse is fully underway. See Figure 11. All about the black disk of the Moon glows the gentle light of the Sun's outer atmosphere, the *corona.* The inner corona will prove most striking in the telescope since it consists of much brighter and rather prominently structured features. The overall shape of the corona is dramatically different when the Sun is near the minimum as opposed to near the maximum of the famous 11-year cycle of solar activity. Near maximum, the corona tends to be more symmetrical; near minimum, the great individual "petals" in the corona elicit comparison to those of a dahlia bloom. It is near minimum that you are more likely to be struck by great "polar brushes" extending from near the top and bottom of the Sun. Many different kinds of structure may be seen in the inner corona—even what seem to be loops in the corona and odd, almost chaotic whirls.

Photographs made with short exposures may reveal these details in the inner corona far better than the eye at the telescope, just as longer exposures may reveal long streamers in the outer corona better. But the eye works admirably over the great brightness range from innermost to outer-

Figure 11 Totally Eclipsed Sun.

most visible corona and thus allows you to survey at least modestly well what several different photograph exposures would be needed to reveal.

Another solar feature, whose appearance at eclipses has struck me as somehow far more vivid, thrilling, and "alive" in the telescope than on the photograph, is the *solar prominence*. These fountainlike formations in the inner corona beyond the Sun's eclipsed surface are solar disturbances shaped by magnetic lines of force. Rarely, one may extend several hundred thousand miles out from the Sun's surface. Admire their vivid orange-red hue and their exquisite shape. Look especially for the kind called a "loop prominence" in which the structure appears to curve all the way back to the solar surface.

The end of totality is one of the most too-soon events in life. Be sure you are keeping track of time and know fairly closely how long totality is supposed to last (there are clues that the end of totality is near, too—like the position of the Moon's shadow if that is prominent in the sky, the ever-greater eclipsing of the prominences at the preceding side of the Moon, and so on). You want to keep track of time so that you get to observe everything you planned to in those never-more-than-few minutes of totality, but also so that you take your eye away from the unshielded telescope and avoid being blinded as the first pieces of photosphere reappear.

Questions

1. What is the overall structure of the corona at this eclipse—more like the solar maximum or the solar minimum form? What individual features do you see in the inner corona? How far out can you trace the outer corona? Can you see any individual streamers out to great distances?

2. How many prominences are visible, and what are their positions on the Sun? What kinds are they?

17.

Darkness and Colors
of Lunar Eclipses

*Note the visibility of various lunar surface features during the
stages of different eclipses. Try to correlate the different levels of
visibility with naked-eye ratings on the Danjon scale. Look for
various colors in different areas of the Moon during stages of the
eclipse. Then use them and your notes on where and when
different parts of the Moon were dark in different degrees to try to
make a darkness and color map of the part of Earth's umbra
through which the Moon passed. Also try to connect any
outstanding anomalies (a very dark eclipse, an unexpected part of
the umbra dark, and so on) with atmospheric occurrences in parts
of Earth.*

Partial lunar eclipses are more easily observable than partial solar eclipses,
and more details are available to observation. Total lunar eclipses are not
such stupendous changes in the ordinary appearance of the whole sky and
landscape as are total solars, nor do they offer the sight of otherwise
unobservable lunar features. But total lunar eclipses (and large partial
ones) do offer remarkable changes in the color and brightness of the Moon
itself and our only chance to survey a large part of a particular thing that is
not the Moon's but our own—Earth's shadow.

The overall color and darkness of the eclipsed Moon (or rather of the
part of Earth's shadow then revealed by our screen Moon) should be
judged by the naked eye, but also by the telescope—an instrument that
can reveal dimmer hues and more details of color than the unaided eye.

The famous Danjon scale of eclipse brightness (see my book, *Seeing
the Sky*, p. 179) is based on naked-eye observations, but the visibility of specific lunar surface features in the telescope offers an alternative (or rather
a complement) to the Danjon method. Only the very darkest eclipses on
record have displayed little or no detail to telescopes. I have found that an
eclipsed Moon with the second lowest whole number, and thus second
darkest, rating on the Danjon scale—L (luminosity) = 1—still permits the
outlines of the major lunar maria (or should we say the bright highlands
that surround them?) to be dimly visible in a typical 6-inch or 8-inch Newtonian reflector. One interesting goal would be to start making detailed

comparisons of Danjon number and visibility of features in telescopes at lunar eclipses so that the telescopic scale could be standardized and correlated with the Danjon scale.

Some of the lovely naked-eye colors of the Moon occur over large enough areas so as to be spread out too much for proper visibility when magnification is used. But other areas of color are either too dim or too small without greater light grasp and magnification. Examples that I have seen on several occasions are a very narrow border of color at the very edge of the *umbra* (the darker, central shadow of Earth) during the midst of the partial phases and touches of color at the extremities of a remaining thin sliver of Moon not covered by the umbra.

The clear message is that we should look at the shadowplay of darknesses and colors on the eclipsed or being-eclipsed Moon with every optical instrument available, if possible—including the naked eye and telescopes. These observations should be carried on during the entire course of each eclipse and at every eclipse (see Table 4), for the Moon's brightness may decrease by as much as a factor of about 4 million during a very dark eclipse or may be about 10,000 times brighter at the middle of a very light eclipse than at the middle of a very dark eclipse.

The situation during the course of each eclipse is more delightfully complex than just a change of brightness that may be either large or truly enormous. Different parts of the Moon will take on different degrees of darkness and different colors in a variety of ways during an eclipse—all because of variations in the conditions of the atmosphere in the band of twilight surrounding Earth at eclipse time. The atmosphere in this band bends sunlight around the edges of the solid Earth so that Earth's shadow is rarely completely dark. It is instead tinted with as great a variety of darkness levels and colors as there is variety in these atmospheric conditions.

So what should be the ultimate aim of your recording of colors and darkness levels at various parts of the Moon and stages of the eclipse? It should be the making of a map of the part of Earth's umbra through which the Moon passed during the eclipse. And, if there are any outstanding anomalies in this map, then you may be able to find the outstanding cause of them in Earth's atmosphere. In July of 1982, the aerosol haze from the El Chichón volcano eruption had not yet spread much into Earth's Southern Hemisphere but had spread to a rather high latitude in Earth's Northern Hemisphere. The Moon was passing almost centrally through the umbra, and, sure enough, it was the northern part of the Moon (thus, of Earth's umbra) that was unusually darkened (except for a thin upper strip corresponding to north polar regions of Earth's atmosphere).

Table 4
Total and Partial Lunar Eclipses, 1991–1999*

Date	Time§	Mag.**	Dir.§§	Dur. Umb.***	Dur. Tot.§§§	Type
1991 Dec 21	10:34	0.09	N	64	—	Partial
1992 Jun 15	4:58	0.68	S	180	—	Partial
1992 Dec 9	23:45	1.27	N	208	74	Total
1993 Jun 4	13:02	1.56	N	218	96	Total
1993 Nov 29	6:26	1.09	S	210	46	Total
1994 May 25	3:32	0.24	N	104	—	Partial
1995 Apr 15	12:19	0.11	S	78	—	Partial
1996 Apr 4	0:11	1.38	S	216	86	Total
1996 Sep 27	2:55	1.24	N	202	70	Total
1997 Mar 24	4:41	0.92	N	202	—	Partial
1997 Sep 16	18:47	1.19	S	196	62	Total
1999 Jul 28	11:34	0.40	N	142	—	Partial

* Data derived from Jean Meeus, *Astronomical Tables of the Sun, Moon, and Planets.* Penumbral lunar eclipses are not included.

§ Ephemeris Time, which for these purposes is virtually identical to Universal Time (see "Note on the Measurement of Time, Position, Angular Distance, and Brightness in Astronomy"). The time given is for mideclipse; if it falls during the night for your location, the eclipse is visible from your area.

** "Magnitude" of eclipse—not brightness here, but the percentage of the Moon's diameter covered with umbra at maximum eclipse. 1.00 (100%) or more is total; "1.27" means the Moon is 1.27 times its own diameter inside umbra.

§§ Direction of Moon from center of umbra at mideclipse. "N" means north of umbra center; "S," south.

*** Duration, in minutes, of umbral eclipse (that is, eclipse during which at least some part of the Moon is in the umbra).

§§§ Duration of total eclipse.

Questions

1. How does a particular total lunar eclipse rate on a scale of telescopic visibility of lunar surface features? How does this scale correlate with that of the famous naked-eye Danjon scale at various eclipses?

2. What colors do you observe on the Moon through the telescope at various stages in a partial lunar eclipse? At various stages in a total lunar eclipse? How might several such hues combine to produce the naked-eye color (or lack of color) in a large part of the Moon?

3. Can you construct from your observations a map of the levels of darkness and colors in the parts of the umbra through which the Moon

passed? (Be sure not to be fooled by contrasting colors or one very bright area making another seem darker than it really is by contrast.)

4. If there are any major anomalies in darkness or color, can you connect them with the major atmospheric conditions in a part of Earth that might be responsible?

18.

Enlargement of Earth's Shadow at Lunar Eclipses

Determine the enlargement of Earth's shadow at various lunar eclipses by making careful timings of when the edge of the umbra crosses what seems to be the center of various lunar craters and other features.

The colorfulness of the Moon during a lunar eclipse is caused by Earth's atmosphere bending light around the solid bulk of the planet, into Earth's shadow, and onto the Moon. It is also the atmosphere that is responsible for another remarkable effect—that of making Earth's umbra larger than it should be.

There are two particularly fascinating things about this enlargement of the umbra. One is that its amount varies from eclipse to eclipse. The other is that scientists are not at all sure how much various factors contribute to the enlargement in any given case.

One factor whose amount of effect on the enlargement *is* precisely calculable is the Moon's distance from Earth at the time of eclipse. That this distance matters has sometimes been overlooked (see letter by W. Nijenhuis that points this out, July 1983 *Sky & Telescope*, p. 3).

The fact remains, however, that it is largely the varying content of Earth's atmosphere in the sunrise–sunset zone encircling Earth that makes the variability in the amount of the enlargement. It must be true that greater than usual quantities of moisture and dust in this zone increase the size of the umbra even more than usual—and yet there are some puzzling discrepancies.

The remarkable total lunar eclipses of July 5–6 and December 30,

1982, (discussed in detail in my earlier Wiley book, *The Starry Room*) are a case in point. The December 30 eclipse was much darker, occurring as it did when the aerosol haze from the eruptions of the El Chichón volcano had become denser and had spread much farther than it had in July. Why then was the enlargement of the umbra 1.7 percent at the December eclipse and 2.0 percent at the July eclipse? The latter's occurring around perigee and the former's near apogee would not account for most of the difference.

These figures were derived from the timings of crater disappearances and reappearances made by several hundred observers who reported their results to *Sky & Telescope*. *Sky & Telescope*'s Roger W. Sinnott suggested (p.387 of the magazine's April 1983 issue) that the explanation might lie in December's eclipse being far less central of a passage through the umbra—"if the outline of the umbra is flattened more than we would expect from the Earth's oblateness" (that is to say, more than could be explained just by the fact that Earth itself is slightly oblate, or slightly flattened in the polar dimension). Why would the umbra be more flattened? Sinnott cited a study by F. Link and Z. Linkova of eclipses between 1889 and 1938, which concluded that such additional flattening of the umbra did occur and could be accounted for by assuming an absorbing dust layer in Earth's atmosphere that was both at higher elevation and denser near the equator than it was near the poles.

This sounds reasonable, but questions still remain about which ingredients and to what degree each of various ingredients contribute to the shadow enlargement. As Sinnott wrote, "The Earth's cloud cover, ozone, and high-level dust from volcanic eruptions and meteor showers are all suspected as agents causing changes in the shadow size from one eclipse to another."

There is clearly still much to be learned about this phenomenon and also, from it, about our atmosphere. The prescription for curing this mystery is to make more observations of it at upcoming eclipses.

The way to determine the umbral enlargement is to compare the observed times that the umbra passes over craters with the times predicted for an atmosphereless Earth (one that would cause no shadow enlargement).

You should have a timepiece accurate to within about a second of the correct time. Before the partial eclipse begins, locate the prominent lunar craters that you are going to use. Now, watch the umbra move onto the lunar disk. The edge of the umbra is much sharper than that of the *penumbra* (Earth's lighter, peripheral shadow) but is not always perfectly sharp. So, you must take the place where there is the most abrupt gradient of shading and follow it. The time that you should note, to the nearest 5 seconds, is the time when this region of most abrupt gradient is crossing the crater's center. You should also, of course, try to note the time when the umbra is first and last seen on the Moon (this can be tricky, especially for the initial appearance, however).

Which craters should you use? Where should you send your results? How will you find out what value for the enlargement of the shadow your timings indicates? ALPO will probably be able to help you. But, over the years, *Sky & Telescope* has made a special point of providing predictions for the crater contacts, encouraging readers to submit their timings, and printing the results—including the figure for the shadow's enlargement. Or at least the magazine has done this for total lunar eclipses widely visible in North America. If you live elsewhere in the world, contact your most likely national astronomical organization for amateurs.

Even if you perform this project completely on your own, with no predicted times for the crater contacts, you should eventually be able to get your data to some individual or organization who can use it. By doing so, you may be playing your part in solving some still very considerable mysteries.

Questions

1. Do you have a listing of the predicted times when the umbra-edge will cross various lunar craters? Whether you have a listing or not, have you made sure before the umbral part of the eclipse begins to identify the craters that you will use?

2. When, to the nearest 5 seconds if possible, do you first see the umbra on the Moon? Last see the umbra on the Moon? What are your times (again, to the nearest 5 seconds) for the passage of the umbra-edge over the center of your selected craters? Is the edge of the umbra very sharp, or must you look carefully to detect where the most abrupt gradient in shading is?

3. Do you know to what individual or organization you can send your results? What figure for the size of the umbral enlargement does the recipient of your results come up with? How does this figure compare with the average derived from a large number of observers?

PLANETS

19.

General Observations of Jupiter

Identify as many belts and zones on Jupiter as possible. Learn to draw properly sketches of Jupiter showing the belts and zones you see by accurately representing any differences in the width, darkness, or internal structure of these features. Judge what colors you see in the different belts and zones.

Some beginners might be surprised to learn which planet usually offers the most features of interest for telescopic observers to see. It is not Venus, whose surface is always hidden in clouds that usually show no structure. It is not Mars, which is too small a planet to see well except when it comes especially close. It is not Saturn, whose rings and globe—striking as they are—normally show only a small amount of detail. The planet is Jupiter. See Figure 12.

Jupiter is not only the largest of the planets in true size, but it is also

Figure 12 Jupiter.

the one whose combination of size and distance usually makes it appear largest as seen from Earth. On the infrequent occasions when Venus gets close enough to loom larger than Jupiter, only a small fraction of Venus's disk is lit. So, even then, there is a larger area of illuminated Jupiter to study.

Our first Jupiter project is to become acquainted with the largest features one can observe on the planet—or, rather, in the planet's clouds, for the only parts of Jupiter we ever see are its outer cloudy layers. The way to become familiar with Jupiter's cloud features is to observe them, of course, but there is a technique for learning to observe them (or any planet's features) that the beginner may not realize is virtually essential. It is to sketch them.

Sketching is more than just a valuable record of what you saw. It improves your ability to see. Added concentration is required to note details accurately enough to render them on paper. This is especially true in planetary observation because planetary features are almost always elusive. They come into really sharp view only briefly now and then during moments of excellent "seeing."

The most prominent features on Jupiter to see and sketch are the dark bands running parallel across Jupiter's bright face. Even a 2- or 3-inch telescope of passable quality can show at least a few of them. These dark bands are called *belts*. The lighter stripes between them are known as *zones*. The belts and zones are cloud features that are stretched out into planet-encircling parallel bands by Jupiter's rotation, which is the most rapid of any planet rotation (less than 10 hours per spin). A look at the belts and zones thus immediately tells you which way the rotational axis of Jupiter is aligned (perpendicular to the belts and zones) and therefore where the polar regions are located.

You can also tell where the poles are and where the equator of Jupiter is by another property of the planet that is quite noticeable in small telescopes—its shape. Jupiter is decidedly *oblate*—that is, its diameter measured from pole to pole is less than its equatorial diameter. Jupiter's equatorial diameter is about 6 percent larger than its polar diameter. Your sketch form's blank globe of Jupiter (prepared in advance before you go out to observe and draw) should therefore not be circular but, rather, shaped in this proportion. A dimension of 50 mm by 47 mm is standard.

One more point about sketching Jupiter and other planets: The proper writing implement is a pencil or, rather, three pencils. To depict the range of shadings on Jupiter, pencils of hard, medium, and soft grade should all be used.

The most prominent of Jupiter's features are usually the South Equatorial Belt and North Equatorial Belt, located to either side of the planet's equator. Numerous belts and zones, as well as many other features, may be seen by a good observer with a medium-sized or large telescope—but these are the province of Activity 21 and its more advanced challenges. Beginners should content themselves with first drawing the prominent belts and zones they can detect and then trying to identify them (see Figure 13 in Activity 21).

Beginners can also note what colors they glimpse in the belts and zones. These may at first seem merely gray and yellow-white, respectively. But further examination (or a larger telescope) should reveal at least a hint of brown (you might even say a slight ruddiness) in the belts and distinctive yellow hues in the zones. Remember, however, that even on nights of good "seeing," color estimates should really be tried only when the planet is fairly high (ideally, over 45° above the horizon).

Speaking of color: the famous Great Red Spot of Jupiter is often very pale in color and often difficult to see. It is located near the edge of the South Equatorial Belt. For thorough details on what it looks like and how to study it, see Activity 22.

Questions

1. How many belts can you observe on Jupiter tonight? Which looks the darkest or otherwise most prominent? What differences in the various belts (width, darkness, internal patterns) can you record on your drawings tonight?
2. What are the precise colors of the various belts and zones?

20.

Apparitions of Jupiter

Observe Jupiter at each stage of its apparition. Examine it as soon as possible after conjunction with the Sun to see what changes in cloud features have occurred since Jupiter was last observable. Try to detect the planet's phase effect around quadrature. Notice stars and other celestial objects that Jupiter nears and then recedes from when it starts and stops retrograde motion. Contrast

Jupiter's larger disk and fully lit appearance at opposition with its smaller disk near conjunction with the Sun and its less-than-full appearance around quadrature.

A planet becomes unviewable for a number of days or weeks when it lies near our line of sight with the Sun (or the extension of that line beyond the Sun). At such times, the planet rises and sets near the Sun in our sky and is overwhelmed by the Sun's light. As Earth and the other planets orbit around the Sun in space, these spells of unviewability recur at regular intervals. The long period of visibility between two such spells is called a planet's *apparition.*

Whether you use a telescope or just the naked eye, you need to understand what time of night a planet rises or sets during different parts of its apparition. But there are also changes in a planet's telescopic appearance as an apparition progresses. Even a veteran observer can benefit from reviewing what special sights are visible at certain pivotal points in an apparition.

Let's follow Jupiter through the course of an apparition. What Jupiter does will serve as a good general example of the behavior of any *superior planet* (any planet farther from the Sun than Earth is).

When Jupiter appears to pass due north or south of (rarely, directly behind) the Sun in our sky, we say that it is in *conjunction with the Sun.* Each day after conjunction, Jupiter will rise sooner and sooner before the Sun. Because Jupiter is bright, we may have to wait only a week or two before we first glimpse it coming up low in the growing light of dawn.

Although "seeing" is generally bad when we look low in the sky, there is special reason to try observing Jupiter with your telescope as soon after conjunction as possible. The reason is that Jupiter has been unviewable for several weeks, and there is no telling what remarkable changes its cloud features may have undergone. Few people want to get up before dawn to see only briefly a typically unsteady image of Jupiter. But what if you could be one of the first, perhaps *the* first under good enough conditions with a good enough telescope, to see a major change in Jupiter? What a tantalizing possibility! You might even make a significant contribution to our knowledge of the planet.

As its apparition progresses, Jupiter keeps rising earlier until it is coming up in the middle of the night and is at its highest around daybreak. Now we say that the planet is at *western quadrature*—that is, 90° of elongation west of the Sun.

The special consequence of this for the planet's telescopic appearance is to have the planet show its greatest *phase effect.* Jupiter is so far from both the Sun and Earth that its sunward face is virtually the same as its earth-ward face, but around quadrature the tiny difference is the greatest and Jupiter appears not quite fully lit. A careful telescopic look reveals a narrow strip of shadow along its western side (the side that points toward Earth's west horizon) or its eastern side if it is at *eastern quadrature* (which occurs much later in the planet's apparition). The shadowed strip is very narrow. The superior planets beyond Jupiter show us even less phase effect than Jupiter; the one superior planet closer to the Sun than Jupiter, Mars, can show a much greater phase effect than Jupiter.

As Earth begins to draw closer to being even in its orbital race with a superior planet like Jupiter, we see the planet appear to halt the eastward or *direct motion* that it has in relation to the background of stars. This is the planet's *stationary point*—the first of two. After reaching this point, the planet appears to drift backward as seen against the background stars—an effect of perspective (the planet does not really reverse its direction of orbital motion!) that you can see demonstrated when your car (representing Earth) passes a slower car (representing a superior planet like Jupiter).

The farther a planet is from Earth, the longer it retrogrades—but the smaller is its "retrograde loop" (the pattern its course traces against the backdrop of stars). No special change in the planet's telescopic appearance is produced when the planet starts to retrograde. But the telescopic observer can enjoy the fascinating sight of the planet pausing and seeming to retreat from the stars (or star clusters or nebulas) just east of it to which it had been drawing ever closer.

In the midst of its spell of retrograding, a superior planet like Jupiter reaches *opposition.* In most respects, this is the best time to observe Jupiter—the time when the planet is biggest (because of its closeness) and visible all night long. The term is derived from the fact that the planet is now located opposite the Sun in the sky: The planet rises at sunset, is highest in the middle of the night, and sets at sunrise.

After opposition, the complements of the events that occurred before take place, in opposite order: The planet halts retrograde motion (reaches its stationary point) and begins direct motion; it reaches eastern quadrature (90° east of the Sun in the evening sky); it becomes lost low in the dusk, setting just after the Sun (the end of the apparition). Then, conjunction with the Sun occurs again, and the whole cycle begins all over again.

For any given planet, the length of time between two conjunctions with the Sun (or the recurrence of one of the other pivotal events in an apparition) is always about the same, and is called the *synodic period.* Jupiter's synodic period is about 399 days (365 days, or one Earth-orbit, plus the 34 days it takes for Earth to make up the additional distance covered by Jupi-

67

ter in that time). But Jupiter is too close to the Sun in the sky to be visible for a few weeks around conjunction with the Sun . . . so an apparition of Jupiter is always somewhat shorter than the synodic period.

Questions

1. How soon after its conjunction with the Sun can you first observe Jupiter? Do you notice any major changes in its cloud features since the previous time (before conjunction) that you saw it?

2. Can you detect the phase effect on Jupiter around quadrature? Can you note what stars or other celestial objects Jupiter pulls close to and then backs away from when it begins (or ends) retrograde motion?

3. Can you observe Jupiter right at opposition? Can you contrast its fully lit appearance then with the less-than-full appearance at quadrature? What differences in visibility of features do you notice when Jupiter is at opposition and closest (therefore bigger) and when it is near conjunction with the Sun and almost farthest (therefore smaller)?

21.

Cloud Features of Jupiter

Observe and sketch the many belts and zones of Jupiter on a night of good "seeing." Look for festoons, garlands, rifts, knots, ovals, and white spots. Examine the South Equatorial Belt and North Equatorial Belt for detail. Look for irregularities, even breaks, in the South Temperate Belt. Monitor the Equatorial Zone for any festoons or other features and for any color changes.

You get Jupiter in the field of view of your telescope and see that its limb (edge) is even and fairly steady. You find that a number of belts are plain even at first glance. This is a night of good "seeing" when even a small telescope may show numerous details in the turbulent atmosphere of the giant planet.

Figure 13 shows the full array of belts and zones of Jupiter, along with their designations. Even under the best of conditions, some of these may

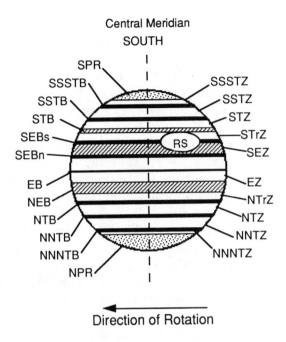

Figure 13 Jupiter's Belts and Zones.

INDEX TO ABBREVIATIONS

ZONES

EZ - Equatorial Zone
SEZ - S. Equatorial Zone
STrZ - S.Tropical Zone
STZ - S.Temperate Zone
SSTZ - S.S. Temp. Zone
SSSTZ - S.S.S.Temp. Zone
NTrZ - N. Tropical Zone
NTZ - N. Temperate Zone
NNTZ - N.N. Temperate Zone
NNNTZ - N.N.N. Temp. Zone

BELTS

EB - Equatorial Belt
SEBn -S. Equatorial Belt North
SEBs -S. Equatorial Belt South
STB - S. Temperate Belt
SSTB - S.S. Temperate Belt
SSSTB-S.S.S. Temperate Belt
NEB - N. Equatorial Belt
NTB - N. Temperate Belt
NNTB - N.N. Temperate Belt
NNNTB - N.N.N. Temp. Belt

OTHER

SPR - S. Polar Region
NPR - N. Polar Region
RS - Great Red Spot

not always be visible because activity in the Jovian atmosphere may subdue them.

The belts and zones appear as bands running parallel with lines of latitude because of the planet's rapid rotation. Although it is about 11 times as wide as Earth, Jupiter completes a full rotation almost 2½ times faster: The largest planet is thus also the fastest spinning. We do not observe a solid surface of Jupiter and so, as in the case of the Sun, Jupiter has a different rotation rate at different latitudes. The difference is not great, but it becomes significant when you are tracking long-lasting features (which, by the way, can also show drift independent of the larger-scale atmospheric flow they are in). We speak of two major regions of different rotation on Jupiter: the areas of System I and System II rotation. System I averages 9 hours, 50 minutes, 30 seconds; System II averages 9 hours, 55 minutes, 40 seconds. System I is confined just to the Equatorial Zone (EZ) and, of course, any features that may appear within this zone. System II includes all latitudes north and south of the EZ.

Before we consider the different kinds of features that you may observe on Jupiter, ponder the consequences of Jupiter's rapid rotation for how sketching of the planet's features must be done.

In sketching Jupiter, you must identify the correct orientation of the planet, which should be as in Figure 13, with south at the top and the direction of rotation from right to left (which is astronomical east to west—the "east" side of Jupiter being the side closer to your east horizon). What must be avoided are telescopes with reversed images (do not use a right-angle prism with the eyepiece of your refractor or Schmidt–Cassegrain).

Jupiter's rotation is so swift that a feature near the center will be at the left edge only 2½ hours later. But to obtain a good view (with little foreshortening), a feature should be at least an hour away from the limb. So, of the 5 hours it takes for a Jovian cloud formation to cross the planet's face, only about 3 hours are suitable for observation and sketching. More importantly, if you are trying to make a sketch, the situation of features changes enough in about 45 minutes to make your drawing seriously in error. You must sketch in the major features quickly, make this the standard time of your drawing, and then, beginning at the left limb where features will be disappearing, add in the less conspicuous or more intricate details.

Besides knowing the time of your observation, it is good to know the Jovian longitude of the central meridian at the time (see the next activity for the importance of this information to studying the Red Spot's drift). You can find this information for the current year in the *Astronomical Almanac* (see the "Sources of Information" section).

Refer back to Activity 19 for more advice on the shape of disk you should draw and type of pencils you should use in sketching Jupiter. Pencils should always be used, but there is a kind of Jupiter sketch that does not require portraying its disk—a *strip sketch*. This is a drawing of a strip of a certain limited latitude range, extended for as long a span of longitude as the observer can watch pass the central meridian of Jupiter during the course of an observing session. (When Jupiter is near opposition within a few months of winter solstice, we can actually observe all longitudes of Jupiter during the course of one long night.)

What types of smaller cloud features can be seen within the belts and zones, and what are the special properties to look for from each of the major belts and zones?

Two reasonably common types of features on Jupiter are *festoons* and *garlands.* They are extensions, usually thin and delicate, into the light zones from out of the dark belts. A festoon bridges the entire width of the zone; a garland does not but may form a hook or curve all the way back to make a closed loop. On the other hand, a *rift* is a bright bridge of cloud spanning from one zone to another across a dark belt.

Ovals are noncircular patches, usually very bright and fairly large. *White spots* are rounder and more sharply defined but relatively small. *Knots* are thickenings (or darkenings) in parts of the belts.

Of all the areas of Jupiter, the South Equatorial Belt (SEB) is often the most prominent and the most active. It is really composed of two belts, a north (SEBn) and a south (SEBs). Festoons and white spots may connect these two. The SEBs is famous for bordering the Great Red Spot, which lies just south of the SEBs and which has interactions with it. The SEB as a whole is also famous for at quite infrequent intervals becoming subdued or even invisible for a number of months (while the Great Red Spot becomes more vivid and colorful) and then bursting back into prominence with much related activity. The Great Red Spot is discussed in detail in the next activity.

The North Equatorial Belt (NEB) is usually wide and prominent. When Jupiter is very active, the NEB occasionally develops lesser and short-lived but reasonably prominent and colorful versions of the Great Red Spot! Typically, more ordinary spots and knots are common in this belt.

The South Temperate Belt (STB) borders the Great Red Spot to the south. It is very irregular (often containing knots and even breaks) and occasionally can be the darkest belt on Jupiter.

The Equatorial Zone (EZ) is frequently crossed by the festoons of the NEB and SEB and is set off nicely by them to permit judgment of its variable hue. Very rarely, an EB (Equatorial Belt) may form within the EZ.

Questions

1. How many of the different smaller-scale features (festoons, ovals, and so on) can you detect on Jupiter tonight? Where are they located? How long do they endure?

2. Which belts are the most prominent on Jupiter tonight? What is the state of the South Equatorial Belt, North Equatorial Belt, and South Temperate Belt?

3. What features are visible within the Equatorial Zone? What is its current color (as well as that of other Jovian features)?

4. Can you produce a strip sketch of some particularly active latitudinal band of Jovian cloud features?

22.

The Great Red Spot

Observe the Great Red Spot, noting its prominence, shape, and color. Watch for interactions between the Spot and other cloud features. Judge the time the Spot transits the central meridian of Jupiter on various nights to determine which way and how much it is drifting in longitude.

The Great Red Spot is the most famous of Jupiter's features and perhaps the most famous "feature" in our solar system unless the rings of Saturn are considered a "feature." Like Saturn's rings, the Great Red Spot has been found to be not entirely unique: Saturn has its Great White Spot break out about once every 30 years, Neptune has a Great Dark Spot, which may be as enduring as Jupiter's Red Spot. And even Jupiter has smaller reddish spots break out in its opposite (northern) hemisphere from time to time. But—again like Saturn's rings—none of the competitors can really come close to rivaling the Great Red Spot's combination of size, color, and endurance.

Considering all this, beginning observers may be surprised to hear of one way in which the Great Red Spot is rather unlike Saturn's rings: The Spot is not often all that easy to see in small telescopes. Be that as it may, whatever the Spot lacks in extreme prominence, it certainly makes up for in complexity and mystery. This peculiar feature is an outstanding object for serious amateur study.

Before examining how to observe the Great Red Spot and what to look for in these observations, we should explore a little bit of the background of known physical facts about the strange feature.

The size and shape of the Great Red Spot vary a bit, but it generally measures about 16,000 miles (26,000 km) east to west by almost 9,000 miles (14,000 km) north to south (compare this with Earth's diameter of just less than 8,000 miles). The Spot rotates (counterclockwise once about every 6 days) and has an upward flow of gases in its center. This sounds like a hurricane on Earth, but conditions on Jupiter are incredibly different from those on our own world. Jupiter's interior produces more heat than it receives from the distant Sun. And, for several reasons (the lack of solid land, the depth of the atmosphere, and so on), the energy of the Spot is not easily dissipated: This "storm" has been in existence at least as long as telescopes became good enough to see it (certainly over a century and a half).

Voyager spacecraft photos show that the Great Red Spot also restores its energy by stealing it from smaller spots and cloud formations. They, and laboratory experiments and computer models, show that the Spot is really most like a vast but shallow whirl being rolled between two powerful currents headed in opposite directions. But tremendous questions remain, not the least of which is, why has only Jupiter's *southern* hemisphere given rise to a Great Red Spot? We do not yet know completely why the Spot behaves as it does; we only suspect that phosphine gives the feature its characteristic color.

The reasons that the Spot's color, prominence, and motion change dramatically from year to year are not really understood—but there is hope, however, that careful observations of the Spot and its environs may provide the information to answer these questions.

The Spot is easy enough to identify if you know where to look. In the last few years, *Sky & Telescope* has (when Jupiter was well-placed for viewing) published predictions of when the Spot would be crossing the planet's central meridian. But of course even when you do not know in advance when the Spot will be transiting the central meridian, you can still look for it by scanning at the appropriate latitude—about 20°S on Jupiter, which happens to be just south of the South Equatorial Belt (SEB). In fact, the Spot overlaps upon the SEB, and activity in one is often closely connected with activity in the other.

The most remarkable outbreak of activity in which these two features share is an infrequent but spectacular one that lasts roughly 1 to 1½ years and that last occurred in 1989–1990. In this monumental disturbance, the SEB loses its prominence (it is usually the most conspicuous feature on Jupiter) but the Red Spot becomes more visible and more colorful—until the boisterous return of the SEB to prominence, at which time the Spot may become very faded and almost colorless.

73

Does the Red Spot ever become so faded as to disappear even in quite large telescopes? Yes, but when this happens, we are left with the then-conspicuous surrounding gap called "the Red Spot Hollow." Is the color really red? Often the Spot is a gray or pale tan, but, when vivid, its hue can be a strong salmon pink.

The changes in the Red Spot's appearance need to be noted in coordination with its interactions with other features. Is there a change in the Spot's appearance when it passes another feature? More fundamentally, why is it passing another feature—that is, is the Spot speeding up or slowing down, and how much is it drifting in longitude? In order to make your own determinations of how much the Spot is drifting, you must be able to time to within a minute when the center of the Spot is transiting the planet's central meridian. A minute's accuracy is easy to obtain with a properly set watch (or by listening to WWV time signals). But how easy is it to judge exactly where the central meridian runs? Fortunately, the prominent exactly east–west belts and zones of Jupiter make not very difficult the task of estimating the meridian running from pole to pole perpendicular to these belts and zones.

But what is the standard against which to determine how much the Great Red Spot is changing longitude? To find what longitude is at the central meridian for any time, you can refer to the tables in the *Astronomical Almanac* (see the "Sources of Information" section). Although the average time it takes for the Great Red Spot to circle the planet is very close to what one would expect of a feature in System II rotation (which, remember, is 9 hours, 55 minutes, 40 seconds), the Spot can vary from this considerably.

A precise determination of the Spot's size can be made by timing when its leading edge and its trailing edge transit the central meridian.

Questions

1. What is the shape and prominence of the Great Red Spot this week? What is its color? If the Spot is too faded to see, what is the shape, prominence, and color of the Red Spot Hollow?

2. Can you detect any interactions between the Great Red Spot and other features? What kind? Do your timings of the Spot's central meridian transits indicate it is drifting east or west in longitude? Faster or slower? What is the precise size of the Spot now as determined by the transit times of its preceding and trailing edges?

23.

The Galilean Satellites and Their Configurations

With a medium-sized telescope on nights of good "seeing," observe the disks of the Galilean satellites when they are away from, near to, and in front of the planet. With a large telescope and excellent "seeing," look for any sign of brightness variations across the tiny disks when they are in these different positions relative to the planet. Examine the color of the satellites under these various circumstances and also when one satellite is very near to another. Look for interesting arrangements of the Galilean satellites, including close conjunctions of moons and such conjunctions when the moons are moving in opposite directions and their movement is directly perceptible.

In the nights that Galileo first turned his little telescope upon Jupiter, he was in for one of the few most astonishing and significant sights he ever beheld. Jupiter showed a disk, of course, but what was at that time still unique was what he saw lined up to either side of the disk—four starlike points of light whose nightly and hourly motions with respect to Jupiter proved that these objects must be none other than moons of Jupiter. Here was unequivocal proof that worlds other than Earth could have moons. Even more importantly, these "Galilean satellites" demonstrated that, at the very least, not *all* permanent bodies in the planetary system revolved around Earth.

The two Voyager flybys of the Galilean satellites over a decade ago gave us close-up looks at these moons that astounded everyone and that answered many questions. Of course, a whole new slew of questions was raised, but these were deeper, more knowledgeable questions, and a successful mission by the Galileo spacecraft (due to reach Jupiter in 1995) could answer them, bringing us a third qualitative leap in understanding to match those made by Galileo (the man) and Voyager.

All of this wonderful surveillance of the Galilean satellites by spacecraft means that there is far less of scientific importance that could conceivably be learned by amateur observations of them. There is still a little opportunity for contribution to science, however. And there is never going to be a time when observation of these moons and their complex dance is not going to be one of the most entertaining and aesthetically satisfying of telescopic endeavors.

The four moons are the only large ones in Jupiter's family of at least 16, but these four really are huge—no other planet has more than a single satellite in this size range. The four, working outward from Jupiter, are Io, Europa, Ganymede, and Callisto. The first two are similar in size to Earth's hefty Moon, but Ganymede and Callisto are, respectively, the first and third largest moons in our solar system, with Ganymede outsizing the planet Mercury. The Voyagers found each of the four a very different marvel, determined in part by how much an ancient surface was transformed by the gravitational effects of Jupiter (and the fellow moons). Thus, Callisto, the farthest out of the four, is almost as heavily peppered with ancient impact craters as a world could possibly be; Ganymede has some cratered regions but also large areas perhaps originally formed in a fashion reminiscent of the plate tectonics that still move vast sections of our own world's crust; Europa is smoothed over with ice, which may conceal an ocean still kept liquid by the tidal energy of nearby Jupiter and the other moons; and Io—incredible Io—is so churned by tidal forces that it keeps erupting from volcanic vents that have perhaps several times in the eons succeeded in turning this moon literally inside out.

To detect the disks of the Galilean satellites is not difficult. To transform them from fat "stars" to tiny but definite disks on a night of good "seeing" (this is a truly fascinating sight) can be achieved with a good 6-inch f/7 Newtonian. Check to find out whether the visibility of the disks is improved when they are seen to pass directly in front of the planet (see the next activity). Better conditions and a larger telescope are surely necessary for any hope of detecting any surface features (variations in light and dark) on the moons. Given the right telescope and night, you should certainly try!

Color is easier. The ruddiness of Callisto has been noted for a very long time by observers, even with quite small instruments. The Galilean satellites are, after all, remarkably bright. They are fourth and fifth magnitude objects when Jupiter is anywhere near opposition. The only reason that naked-eye sightings of them are rare is the glare of stupendously brighter Jupiter nearby (I have seen Ganymede and Callisto naked-eye myself but am a little skeptical about reports of the closer-to-Jupiter moons Europa and Io having been spotted without optical aid). In any case, their brightness makes what color they do display accessible to a fairly small telescope.

Try rating the color both with and without Jupiter in the field of view and also with the moon right in front of the disk of Jupiter to see what influence the planet's own color and brightness have on your estimates of the moons' hues. Look carefully on nights of excellent "seeing," especially when two Galilean satellites are near each other. Although color contrast exaggerates the hues of celestial objects that appear very near each other (double star components are the famous example), this bias can be taken into account.

Easiest of all is to enjoy the movements and various patternings of the Galilean satellites. A few hours, even a few minutes, can dramatically change their pattern. At high magnification, the motions of two heading in opposite directions but appearing near the same line of sight become directly detectable. A particular arrangement you see tonight may not be repeated for a very long time. Look for close conjunctions of two or three moons, double conjunctions (two pairs of two moons), Callisto north or south of Jupiter, and all the moons on one side. The rare sight of Jupiter "without visible satellite" and many other possibilities raised by the occurrence of transits, eclipses, occultations, and shadow transits are discussed in our next activity.

Questions

1. What is the smallest telescope with which you can certainly detect the actual disks of the Galilean satellites (both when in front of the planet and away from it)? Can you ever glimpse any brightness variations (surface detail) on any of the moons with a large telescope and excellent "seeing"?

2. What is the color of each of the Galilean satellites (when in front of Jupiter and when viewed with the planet out of the field of view)? What is the color of each when seen in close conjunction with one another?

3. What interesting arrangements of Jupiter's moons (all on one side, close conjunctions, and so on) can you observe and draw? Can you detect immediately perceptible motion in the moons when they are in conjunction and heading in opposite ways?

24.

Eclipse Phenomena of the Galilean Satellites

Watch the Galilean satellites engage in eclipses, occultations, transits, and shadow transits with Jupiter. Compare the sizes and colors of the moons and their shadows during these events. If you wish, join other amateur astronomers in making rigorous timings of the eclipse disappearances and reappearances of the satellites.

The bright, large Galilean satellites circle Jupiter in orbits that are inclined only a little to the planet's equatorial plane. Jupiter's equatorial plane is inclined only a little to the plane of its orbit. The orbit of Jupiter is inclined only a little to the orbit of Earth. The result of these three facts is that, each year, observers on Earth can see dozens of passages of the moons in front of and in back of Jupiter, as well as dozens of passages of the moons through Jupiter's shadow and the moons' shadows across Jupiter.

Actually, some of the events are rather difficult to see, even with medium-sized telescopes. It is generally easier to see the dark shadow of a moon go across the bright face of Jupiter than it is to see the moon itself as it passes in front of this face. Any of the events require at least moderately good "seeing" to observe properly. There are also periods when some of these events do not occur. For instance, there are long spells when the outermost of the four moons, Callisto, passes north or south of the planet. And around opposition, the shadow of Jupiter lies almost completely behind it as viewed from Earth so that any moon passing into this shadow has already disappeared from our view behind the planet anyway (the time when the eclipses by Jupiter's shadow occur longest before or after a moon goes behind the planet is around quadrature, for a definition of which, see Activity 20).

Despite these limitations, a careful observer with a medium-sized telescope can expect a shot at seeing at least one, sometimes several, of the eclipse, occultation, transit, or shadow events of the Galilean satellites on most nights when Jupiter is visible for quite a few hours.

Now look at Figure 14. Let's give the four kinds of phenomena their proper names and abbreviations. The event in which a satellite passes behind the planet is an *occultation* (Oc). The event of passing in front of the planet is a *transit* (Tr). The event of passing through the shadow of the planet is an *eclipse* (Ec). The shadow of a moon passing in front of the

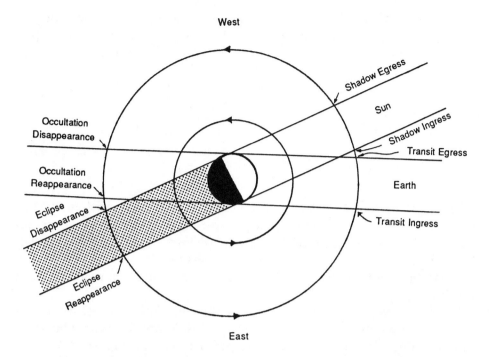

West

East

Figure 14 Explanation of Galilean Satellite Phenomena. Globe is Jupiter's. Zones marked "Sun" and "Earth" are lines of sight from Sun and Earth, respectively. These lines of sight often coincide more closely than shown in the particular situation of the diagram. When they coincide closely, eclipses occur during occultations and therefore cannot be observed (see text).

planet—that is, seen projected on the bright clouds of Jupiter—is a *shadow transit* (Sh).

There are more terms and abbreviations used to describe the beginnings and ends of these events: The start of a transit or shadow transit is *ingress* (I), and its end is *egress* (E); the start of an eclipse or occultation is *disappearance* (D), and its end is *reappearance* (R). Finally, there are the Roman numeral designations of the Galilean satellites: I = Io, II = Europa, III = Ganymede, and IV = Callisto.

You will need to know these abbreviations and numeral designations when you are consulting any listing of the Galilean satellite events for a month or year (such shorthand is necessary because there are so many events, although many will not occur with Jupiter up or the sky dark at your location). Handy sources of these events are the *Astronomical Almanac* and the yearly *Observer's Handbook of the Royal Astronomical Society of Canada* (see the "Sources of Information" section). The "corkscrew" diagrams

79

of the moons in *Sky & Telescope* and *Astronomy* magazines are not precise but give a rough idea of when events will occur. A typical listing for a particular date in the *Almanac* or *Observer's Handbook* might read as follows:

8 40	I. Oc.D.
12 02	I. Ec.R.
13 22	II. Oc.D.
18 23	II. Ec.R.
23 52	IV. Tr.I.

The initial numbers in each entry are the UT (Universal Time). The events would be an occultation disappearance of Io, an eclipse reappearance of Io, an occultation disappearance of Europa, an eclipse reappearance of Europa, and a transit ingress of Callisto. (Can you picture what is happening with Io and Europa? Why are their occultation reappearances not listed?)

These predictions are surprisingly difficult, and some of the major publications use an ephemeris that can be considerably in error. The gravitational pulls of the Galilean satellites perturb one another. And, in practice, several uncertainties may affect the timing of your observation: The angle at which a satellite enters Jupiter's shadow, or passes behind or before it, does vary a little bit—and this is important because when a Galilean satellite reappears to telescopic view there is already some of it out of eclipse (likewise, when you see it disappear in eclipse, there is still part of the moon not yet in Jupiter's shadow). The larger the telescopic aperture you have, the longer you should be able to follow a Galilean satellite as it fades into eclipse. The accuracy of timing an observation is further complicated by the fact that the Sun as seen from out near Jupiter still does have a sizable (though small) disk and therefore causes a lighter peripheral shadow or penumbra (a term familiar to all who have studied eclipses of our own Moon).

Although getting accurate times of these Galilean satellite events has been difficult for both predictor and observer, the need to obtain such times is important if we are to understand the gravitational workings of the Jovian system, which forms a convenient and far swifter model of our entire solar system and its gravitational perturbations and orbital evolutions. Fortunately, the first spacecraft flybys of Jupiter made possible a new JPL (Jet Propulsion Laboratory) ephemeris of Galilean satellite events; and, in 1976, *Sky & Telescope* editor Joseph Ashbrook launched an amateur project (recruiting large numbers of amateur astronomers) to time Galilean satellite eclipses, which was taken up by ALPO and carried on by John

Westfall after Ashbrook's death in 1980. Such increased accuracy was useful to plans for the Galileo spacecraft mission. For a large article on the topic of timing the eclipses, see the August 1984 issue of *Sky & Telescope*, pp. 181–184. The magazine and ALPO are still interested in observers who want to perform these timings.

Presumably, after the Galileo spacecraft begins its studies of Jupiter and the Jovian system in 1995, the scientific need for amateur timings of eclipses will decrease. But the fascination of watching these moons slowly nudge into eclipse or out, gradually drift behind the giant planet's globe, or creep across the face of Jupiter—sometimes chasing (or chased by) their own or another moon's shadow—that captivation will never cease.

The Jovian system is so complex that you will never see anything like every combination possible even in a lifetime. Some combinations are impossible—for instance, Io, Europa, and Ganymede can never all three be in transit at once or in eclipse at once. Some combinations are very rare. Roger W. Sinnott found that Jupiter is "without visible satellite" (all four Galilean satellites either in eclipse, occultation, or transit) just 20 times, for a total of 15.8 hours, in the entire twentieth century. The last such event was in January of 1991; the next will not be until August 27, 1997.

Questions

1. Can you observe each of the Galilean satellites in transit, shadow transit, eclipse, and occultation? What can you note about the relative visibilities of these events and of each of the satellites in them? How often can you compare two moons simultaneously in transit, or a moon and a shadow, and so on?

2. Do you wish to join other amateurs in timing rigorously the eclipse disappearances and reappearances of Galilean satellites? What differences in duration of visibility do you note with telescopes of different size?

25.

Apparitions of Venus—Part 1

Observe the disk of Venus as soon after superior conjunction as possible. Note when you first can tell that its phase is gibbous.

Look for subtle cloud features and deformations of the planet's terminator when it is still a large gibbous (a time when few observers look). Look for these characteristics especially carefully around the time when Venus is half lit. Notice how many days before greatest eastern elongation you think Venus is perfectly half lit.

Venus is by far the brightest planet and comes much closer to Earth than any other—close enough to appear larger than any planet, even larger than giant but distant Jupiter. And yet, despite all this, Venus is often a difficult planet to observe telescopically and usually shows less detail than Jupiter, Saturn, or Mars. In fact, it often shows no detail!

That such a bright, huge, and close object should be so sparing of visual information makes it and its consequent mysteries all the more tantalizing. That such an object should be so sparing also calls for some explanation.

Some of the difficulty in getting a good telescopic view of Venus involves its proximity to the Sun. Venus orbits at only 72 percent of Earth's distance from the Sun, and consequently we never can see it more than 47° from the Sun in the sky. A sizable fraction of the time, it lingers deeply enough in the solar glare to make observation difficult. But the greater problem for telescopic observers is getting a look at Venus when it is high enough to avoid the poor "seeing" we encounter when we look low in the sky (when there is more turbulence because we look down a longer pathway through Earth's atmosphere). Now, it is true that Venus can be seen high in the sky in the middle of the day and that this is actually a better time to look at it anyway because the "surface" (actually cloud) brightness of Venus is so great. (We have a better chance of seeing detail on it against the bright daytime sky than we do against the dark of night upon which it appears too dazzling.) But finding even an object as brilliant as Venus in broad daylight is usually very difficult for those who do not know how to go about it and requires some work even for the veteran observer.

There is a more fundamental problem with seeing detail in the image of Venus. The fact is that the planet is eternally shrouded in cloud and that cloud shows generally few and subtle features. This cloud long prevented all attempts to learn what conditions were like on this closest of Earth's neighbors, which is nearly Earth's twin in size. Only radar and spacecraft missions to Venus have permitted us to discover some of what is below the cloud, as well as what the cloud is and why there are so seldom even the slightest rifts in it.

The yellow cloud-cover of Venus that we see in our telescopes is a layer of sulfuric acid haze very high above the crushingly heavy, predominantly carbon dioxide atmosphere of the planet. The tremendous amounts of carbon dioxide in the Venus atmosphere produce a "greenhouse effect" (solar radiation gets in, but the heat it generates cannot escape) that is immensely stronger than the one with which humanity's fossil fuel burning now threatens Earth. Though twice as far from the Sun as Mercury is, Venus is even hotter; its day bakes with temperatures of around 900° F. Each day lasts slightly longer than the planet's year (the Venus-day is 243 Earth-days long, while the Venus-year is 225 Earth-days long!), and Venus spins backward—that is, it rotates in the opposite direction from the other planets (counterclockwise as seen from above its "north" pole). How the strange rotation came to be is an integral question in our attempts to understand the nature of this hellish world of blistering heat, crushing atmosphere, sulfuric acid cloud-layer, and probable volcanic activity laced with (volcano-caused) lightning.

In several of the following activities, we will see how dedicated visual observers could still conceivably help us resolve some of the outstanding mysteries of Venus. But our present activity is about becoming familiar with how the planet proceeds through an apparition and about what special observational possibilities occur at different points in this apparition.

Venus apparitions fall first into two classes: those in which Venus is the *Evening Star* (visible after sunset in the evening sky) and those in which Venus is the *Morning Star* (visible before sunrise in the morning sky). Although these are almost always two separate periods of visibility, the full cycle of Venus-appearances is not complete (Venus is not back in the same position relative to Earth and Sun) until both apparitions are run through.

Figure 15 assists in understanding the situation and both how and why the situation differs from that of a *superior planet* (planet farther from the Sun than Earth is) like Jupiter. Venus is an *inferior planet* (planet closer to the Sun than Earth is).

Let's begin with the less interesting start to a Venus apparition, the one that begins an evening apparition. When a superior planet is at conjunction with the Sun, the planet must always be on the opposite side of the Sun from Earth. But an inferior planet can have conjunction with the Sun on either the far side or the near side of the Sun from us (in the latter case, it lies directly, or almost directly, between Earth and the Sun). An inferior planet reaches *superior conjunction* on the far side of the Sun from us; it reaches *inferior conjunction* on the near side of the Sun to us. The less interesting start of an apparition is the evening one because it starts after superior conjunction—when Venus is farthest and therefore appears smallest.

Low in the dusk, we see Venus as a round, little disk hardly more than 10 arc-seconds across, which is less than one-third the minimum diameter that Jupiter attains. But *is* it round? The phase effect that for Jupiter was

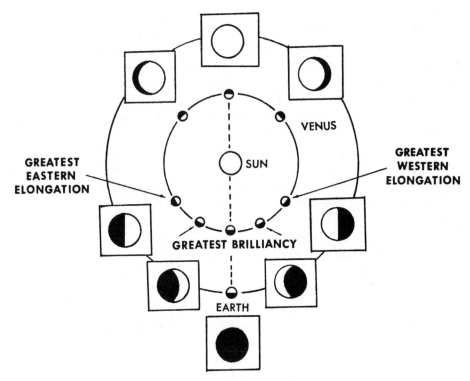

Figure 15 Phases of Venus. Diagrams in the boxes show appearance of Venus as seen from Earth when Venus is in the various orbital positions shown.

scarcely noticeable at best grows ever greater for Venus as the months after superior conjunction pass. Like the other inferior planet (Mercury), Venus goes through a full set of phases as seen from Earth. This is considerable compensation for the difficulty of seeing any cloud features in the pall of Venus—for by its phase we can see at a glance just where Venus must be in its orbital journey in relation to Earth.

Do not neglect to make at least occasional observations of the gibbous Venus. All too many an observer will wait until Venus nears its critical half-lit phase to start watching, and it is quite possible that some interesting sights are being missed. The subject of Activity 27, Schroter's Effect, is harder to determine before half-Venus, but observations of it on the gibbous Venus might be revealing (very few observers try this).

Schroter's Effect and irregular deformations of the terminator are very striking around the time when Venus is half lit, and, although one must guard against spurious appearances caused by optical and (Earth-) atmospheric effects, at least Venus appears half lit near the time when it is at *greatest elongation*—its largest apparent angular separation from the Sun, which is likely to be fairly near the time when it is highest in the sky at sunset (sunset, or sunrise, is a good compromise time of day to observe Venus if you do not want the work of locating it in the daytime, but you do want to see it against a reasonably bright background).

An intriguing fact is that Venus ought to appear half lit exactly at greatest elongation, but usually it appears so at least several days before in the evening apparition. We will study this in more detail in Activity 27.

In an evening apparition, this time of largest angular separation is that of greatest eastern elongation, and it signals the start of a period of intense interest for Venus-observers. We will look at the rest of the evening apparition, and the morning apparition that follows, in our next activity.

Questions

1. How soon after superior conjunction can you get your first telescopic view of Venus, appearing at its smallest and most nearly full? How soon after superior conjunction can you first detect a phase effect on Venus? How much do your "seeing" conditions for Venus improve as the planet's sunset altitude increases in the months after superior conjunction?

2. What cloud features or deformations of Venus's terminator do you notice in your observations of the planet when its phase is gibbous? When the planet is half lit? How many days before greatest elongation do you judge Venus to be exactly half lit? (See Activity 27 for more details on this observation.)

26.

Apparitions of Venus—Part 2

Observe the crescent of Venus as it approaches inferior conjunction, looking for the Ashen Light and cusp-caps. View the thinnest, tallest crescent Venus you can as closely before and after inferior conjunction as possible. After inferior conjunction, follow the phases of Venus and the appropriate observations in reverse order. Determine how many days after greatest elongation you think

Venus is exactly half lit. Try to observe Venus as closely before superior conjunction as possible.

We left off in the previous activity with greatest eastern elongation, the beginning of a time of dramatic changes in both the sky-positioning and the telescopic appearance of Venus.

After months of the slow decrease in illuminated fraction and slow increase in apparent diameter, the globe now rapidly enlarges even as its illuminated portion dwindles to narrowness. When it is about one-third illuminated, we get (to explain it a little simplistically) the compromise of these two trends, which gives the greatest surface area—and therefore the greatest total brightness. The technical term *greatest brilliancy* is used and corresponds in the case of Venus almost but not quite with the time of maximum brightness. Then, Venus is becoming an ever larger but skinnier crescent. Its shape is visible even in binoculars—maybe occasionally even to the naked eye! But the planet is simultaneously losing elongation, and therefore altitude in the sunset or after-sunset sky, very rapidly.

A look back at Figure 15 helps show why. Venus at this time has "rounded the corner" of its orbit and is heading ever more laterally in space with respect to Earth—a lateral motion that will bring it between us and the Sun. It is not just the increasingly lateral component of its motion with respect to Earth that makes Venus set so drastically sooner and sooner after the Sun each night. It is also Venus's greater apparent speed, which is caused by the fact that it is getting so much closer to Earth.

At this time, a large portion of Venus that is facing Earth is the nighttime part. Occasionally, however, observers have seen a dim glow across this nighttime part. It is the Ashen Light, which we will consider in more detail in Activity 29.

The race is on between the thinning of the crescent and its lengthening (smaller cloud features would appear large enough to be visible, but ever less of the giant globe is now illuminated). The race is between the approach of the planet toward Earth (desirable for observations) and the approach of the planet toward our line of sight with the Sun (undesirable for observations). In Activity 30, we will discuss some of the special observations visible in this breathtaking time.

The race is lost for the observer when Venus gets so near the Sun and sets so soon after sundown that it cannot be observed (actually, in rare cases, there is a chance of observing Venus each day straight through until it appears on the morning side of the Sun). The evening apparition is over. Venus now goes through inferior conjunction (almost always a little north or south of the Sun, not right across the Sun's face).

How many days before inferior conjunction was Venus too low at sunset to see? The answer to this question depends on the observer, the weather, and other obvious factors. But it also depends greatly on what time of year this is occurring, especially if you observe at middle latitudes on Earth, because at different times of year Venus will be farther north than the Sun on the zodiac (favorable for Northern-Hemisphere observers), and the zodiac (or its midline, the Sun's path, the ecliptic) makes a steeper angle with the sunset or dusk horizon. For the Northern Hemisphere, the angle of the ecliptic around sunset is steepest around the spring equinox so that, whatever the angular separation of Venus from the Sun may be, the separation is transformed almost entirely into angular altitude vertically above the setting Sun.

At mid-northern latitudes, the best time of year for Venus to shoot up a steep section of zodiac in the dawn sky after inferior conjunction is around the autumn equinox. But whether this section is steep or shallow with respect to the dawn horizon, Venus will progress up the section after inferior conjunction and rise sooner and sooner before the Sun. The first sighting of Venus on the morning side of the Sun is the beginning of the morning apparition. The observations of the crescent Venus from before inferior conjunction are again possible but this time in the opposite order—from thinnest crescent, back to greatest brilliancy, and onward to greatest *western* elongation. It is a few days after greatest elongation in the morning that Venus generally looks half lit (check how many days at this particular apparition).

During a morning apparition, you can find Venus more easily in broad daylight—by not losing it. Simply keep it in your field of view until after sunrise.

After greatest western elongation, the excitement of observing Venus quiets. But as the months of slow shrinking of disk size and increase of illuminated fraction wear on, we should not abandon the planet entirely. Whenever you are up for dawn observations, try to fit at least a quick look at Venus into your program until superior conjunction claims it again, at about 584 days (about 19½ months) after that event's last occurrence.

Questions

1. Do you notice the Ashen Light on any nights as Venus's illuminated fraction diminishes? When is the planet's crescent first large enough (tall enough) to see in your finderscope or binoculars? Do you see any deformations of the crescent-tips (cusps), such as cusp-caps?

2. How close before inferior conjunction can you observe Venus? What are its elongation and illuminated fraction then? How soon after sundown does it set? What are the figures for these that you achieve in your first sighting of Venus in the morning sky after inferior conjunction?

3. How many days after greatest western elongation do you think that Venus is exactly half lit? What deformations of the planet's terminator and cloud features can you see around this time and then after (when the planet is gibbous)? How soon before superior conjunction can you view Venus?

27.

Dichotomy of Venus and Schroter's Effect

Try to establish the existence of and amount of Schroter's effect at the phases of Venus other than half-Venus. Record the probabilities of the Venus terminator being straight, concave, and convex for many days before and including greatest evening elongation, as well as for many days after and including greatest morning elongation. Determine the number of days before or after greatest elongation that dichotomy occurs, using several telescopes and noting "seeing" and other observing conditions. Compare your results from different apparitions to see how much the lapse between greatest elongation and dichotomy varies, specifically between various apparitions and generally between morning versus evening apparitions.

The phases of Venus are easy to see; the cloud features, difficult at best. But the latter appear to have a striking effect on the former, an effect that the amateur with a small, good telescope can study and perhaps even increase our knowledge of Venus by.

If the Venus we saw were a smooth-surfaced solid ball, its phases would appear as expected from straightforward geometric considerations. Instead, we see the clouds of Venus, which are less strongly lit (and lit less deeply into) by the slanting sunlight near the terminator on Venus. We therefore do not quite see to the true boundary of light and dark on the planet. Consequently, a phase of Venus looks slightly smaller than it should.

Very careful studies of this—*Schroter's effect*—might tell us more about the clouds (and atmosphere?) of Venus than we yet know. But precise enough sketching of the planet is difficult, especially when Venus is far and small, as its phase is when it is a gibbous of, say, 75 percent or more (75 percent of the diameter along the equator illuminated). We should try to do such sketching, especially at the 70-percent or 60-percent phase, a time when such work is still largely neglected by most amateur astronomers. Most observers are lazy enough to wait until the 50-percent, or half-Venus, phase. Indeed, this phase does warrant special attention for a very special reason: The eye's ability to detect deviations from a straight line is very good, and, when Venus appears exactly half lit, its terminator should appear as a straight line.

Now, we should remember that this straight line should be perfectly straight only in the sense of not being concave or convex as a whole. There may still be small individual deformations of the terminator. These are often seen in observations of Venus at any phase, and, when they are real (not a result of the limitations of your optical aid or of Earth's turbulent atmosphere), they must represent darker and lighter, more or less dense areas in the Venus cloud-cover. Actually, the vagaries of Earth's atmosphere are such that you may have to rate at each observation near greatest elongation (the time when a smooth, billiard-ball Venus would be 50 percent lit) the percentage of the three probabilities that the terminator is straight, convex, and concave.

The condition in which Venus appears to be exactly half lit, its terminator neither convex nor concave but straight, is called *dichotomy*. And, due to the clouds of Venus, dichotomy generally occurs a few days before greatest elongation (evening sky) and a few days after greatest western elongation (morning sky).

The interesting thing here is that the amount of time between dichotomy and greatest elongation seems to vary from one apparition to another and to generally be longer in the evening sky. The lapse between dichotomy and greatest elongation at evening apparitions can be as great as 8 to 10 days; at morning apparitions, only as great as 4 to 6 days. (Sometimes, the values are much less than these two sets of figures.) These differences from one apparition to another seem to be borne out by relatively good agreement among skilled observers. The question is whether they could still arise from some earthly cause or whether they represent changes in Venus's clouds. The latter seems highly likely.

By the way, although certain filters may be of help in studying Venus, the estimates of dichotomy that you make and that will be compared with those of other observers should be made without filters.

Questions

1. Can you verify the existence of Schroter's effect on Venus at phases other than half-Venus by comparing your careful sketches to the predicted percentage illuminated in publications like the *Astronomical Almanac?* What is its amount at various phases?

2. How many days before greatest evening elongation and after greatest morning elongation do you behold dichotomy? How much does this vary at different apparitions? Between evening and morning apparitions in general? Do you get different figures for when dichotomy occurs with different sizes of telescopes? How much does a given degree of "seeing" (on a 1-to-5 or a 1-to-10 scale) affect the percentage of probability you can assign to the dominant possibility between straight, convex, and concave terminator?

28.

Cloud Features of Venus

Study any markings that you think you glimpse on the disk of Venus. Try to observe with different telescopes and different observers, evaluate "seeing" conditions, and otherwise help to distinguish between spurious markings and those that represent true cloud features of Venus. Test how much better your results are when you are observing Venus high in broad daylight as compared to in a sunset, twilight, or nighttime sky. Try to see whether you can ever chart the progress of certain cloud features in their rapid circling of the slowly backward-spinning planet.

The deformations and darker areas frequently seen near the terminator of Venus, whatever the planet's phase may be, are tantalizing. But the observer must be very careful in assessments of the probability that such features are really in the clouds of Venus. Often, the markings near the terminator and other parts of the planet are contrast effects or other results of some combination of less-than-ideal optics and less-than-ideal "seeing." The glare of Venus in even a twilight sky produces ghost images, and even with clean telescopic optics much light is still scattered within the eye itself.

For all these problems, observing Venus high in broad daylight is one of the best solutions. How do you find it? With accurate setting circles and polar alignment, you can dial (or with computer-assisted telescope drive, you can gently fingertip-punch) your way to the position of Venus that you have looked up in the *Astronomical Almanac* or in one of the astronomy magazines (the latter give the planet's positions for only a few times in the month, so you must interpolate between positions). But, if your telescope is not permanently mounted, you will need to find your bearings by locating the Sun (safely, as discussed in Activity 12). As a matter of fact, if you have the positions of both the Sun and Venus, you can offset from the Sun (*x* number of degrees and minutes of declination north or south, *y* number of hours and minutes of right ascension east or west) and look into your telescope to find Venus there. (Be very careful in this practice never to become confused and look in to discover that the Sun is what is in your field of view!) But suppose that you do not have the necessary equipment or do not want to go through these steps? Under favorable conditions (a very clear sky and Venus at a rather large elongation from the Sun), the practiced scanner can estimate about where Venus should be in relation to the sun and can use an RFT (rich-field telescope), binoculars, or even the naked eye to find it and position it just above a tree or building so that it can be gotten into the main telescope (obviously, you can also try scanning and locating it in your finderscope). By the way, remember that in naked-eye searches of this kind it is crucial to keep your gaze focused on infinity and not on nearby objects as it is wont to be.

Other aids to observing Venus include filters, although each of several kinds used for Venus has its benefits and drawbacks. Wratten #25 filters (red) can improve the contrast between the planet and sky; Wratten #47 (violet) can improve the sharpness. Although ultraviolet photography of Venus is a subject beyond the scope of this book, I would like to mention a possibility that I have considered but not yet tried—visual observations of Venus with a filter that lets through wavelengths only in what is usually considered the near-ultraviolet range. I know people who can see wavelengths shorter than the 390 or 400 nm often suggested as the limit for human vision. Mariner spacecraft photos taken with a 355-nm filter show much Venus cloud detail, including the recurring giant Y pattern. Might some observers, especially those with young eyes (or those with old eyes from which the age-yellowed and cataracted lenses have been removed), be able to see at this wavelength?

When you have done all you can to improve your view of Venus, the reality of whatever cloud features you think you see must be evaluated. Are they visible in different telescopes and by different people? The ultimate goal is to demonstrate that the same features have been followed around the planet. Although a point on the surface of Venus takes a remarkable 243 Earth-days to complete one rotation around the planet, the cloud features move with tremendous swiftness. The spacecraft photos show that they race around the planet in a period of about 4 Earth-days! These winds have been implicated in theories attempting to explain the strange backward rotation of the planet. If you can follow any of the exceedingly subtle markings, you are dealing with the very stuff by which some of Venus's great mysteries may someday be solved.

Questions

1. How often can you establish that markings you see on Venus are cloud features and not contrast effects or other spurious effects produced by the telescope and less-than-ideal "seeing"? Can you do this by getting similar views of them in different telescopes and from different observers on the same day? And by getting different views (a different pattern or position of the pattern) on other days?

2. How much improvement of results do you obtain from observing with Venus high in broad daylight as opposed to just before sunset, or in twilight, or at night? How much improvement do you obtain from any filters you use?

3. Are you ever able to make a case for observing the movement of the same cloud features around the globe of Venus in the period of 4 Earth-days established by spacecraft ultraviolet images?

29.

The Ashen Light

Look for the Ashen Light whenever a sizable portion of the night side of Venus is presented. Note the telescopes, "seeing" and transparency, and any other relevant data for all negative and positive observations. In seeing the Ashen Light, try to determine how its appearance varies (if at all) with different magnifications, telescopes, and observers. Try to establish whether there is any correlation between frequency of sightings of the Light and the particular phase of Venus or kind of apparition (morning or evening). Notice how, or whether, the Light varies in intensity over a spell of minutes or hours. If you have filters, find out what affect they have on the visibility of the Light.

After greatest evening elongation, about 5 weeks elapse between each of the next exciting events in Venus's approach to, passage of, and recession from Earth and the Earth–Sun line. The order of events is as follows: greatest evening elongation, greatest evening brilliancy, inferior conjunction, greatest morning brilliancy, and greatest morning elongation. During this entire period, Venus is technically a crescent. And during this period, there are some special telescopic sights to look for besides aiming for superlatives in seeing Venus the tallest, thinnest, closest to Earth in space, or closest to the Sun in the sky possible.

One legendary phenomenon that Venus is the only planet to display to visual observers on Earth is the *Ashen Light*. Although "legendary," it is also real in the sense that some phenomenon—whether it be on Venus, in Earth's atmosphere, or in observers' eyes or telescopes—is involved. We are all familiar with sometimes seeing the night side of the Moon dimly lit when the Moon is a crescent, and we know (or can learn from astronomy books) that this is *earthshine*, the light of Earth illuminating the lunar surface. But what are we to make of the observations of a glow on the night part of Venus? Venus has no moon to shine on it, and Earth (though nearly at its brightest as seen from Venus when Venus is a crescent in our skies) could not be bright enough to produce this glow.

The three explanations of the Ashen Light are (1) that it is observers' imaginations, (2) that it is caused by lightning associated with volcanic activity on Venus, and (3) that it is an auroral phenomenon of Venus.

There have been enough reliable observers of the Light over the past third of a millennium to ensure that the first theory, mere imagination, is unlikely to be correct (but surely the possibility of a peculiar physiological or Earth-atmospheric cause fooling all these observers is still tenable?). The second theory has its possibilities, although contemporary volcanic activity and accompanying lightning on Venus have apparently not yet been proven quite to everyone's satisfaction. The third theory seems most intriguing perhaps because of, not in spite of, the fact that Venus does not have a magnetic field like the other planets. Might the Ashen Light be a result of solar particles interacting with the gases high in Venus's atmosphere?

A worldwide attempt to verify and explain the Ashen Light was conducted by John L. Phillips and Christopher T. Russell in a period of 240 days centered around the planet's inferior conjunction of June 13, 1988. The results were reported in the January 1990 issue of *Sky & Telescope* (p. 108). They were far less conclusive than hoped. The existence of the Light as more than imagination at least seemed strongly supported by the fact that 30 of the 70 observers making the 700 useful observations did report seeing the Light at least once. A few other significant conclusions were reached. For instance, the Light apparently could vary in intensity rapidly enough to appear in a matter of minutes in a telescope after a negative observation. If the Light actually is more visible in evening apparitions than in morning ones, or at certain phases than at others, the proof was veiled—that is, may have been veiled: The only strong correlation was between number of reports of the Light and number of observers viewing. And there was apparently no correlation between the number of Ashen Light sightings and the electric, magnetic, charged-particle, or ultraviolet-intensity measurements recorded at Venus by the Pioneer Venus Orbiter.

Did filters help make the Light more visible? Some observers saw the Ashen Light directly and found that a filter made it disappear, while others had the opposite experience of the Light's becoming more apparent when a filter was tried. (The filters employed were usually blue or violet.)

Was there a single type of appearance that the Ashen Light had? No, most observers who reported it saw the Light as either a uniform or as a mottled illumination. But a few people saw isolated bright spots. See Figure 16.

The mystery remains. Phillips and Russell recommend a consistent viewing method and suggest continuous recording of the planet with a CCD camera "of appropriate sensitivity and dynamic range on a moderate-size telescope." But perhaps just persistent and careful viewing of Venus by a visual observer can turn up the clue needed.

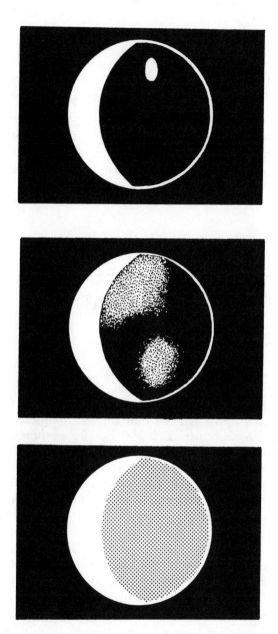

Figure 16 The Ashen Light—Three Different Appearances. (Adapted from diagrams of Phillips and Russell, January 1990 *Sky & Telescope.*)

Questions

1. Can you observe the legendary Ashen Light? How frequently do you see it? Do you notice any correlation between the frequency of your sightings and the particular phase of Venus or any other factor?

2. Does the intensity of the Light vary from one (positive) observation of it to the next? Does it vary in the matter of minutes or hours during which one is observing one night? How does the quality of the "seeing" affect the Light's visibility? How does the use of filters affect it?

30.

Special Observations of Crescent Venus

Look for cusp-caps, and, if you see one, try to establish its reality as an effect not caused by telescope optics or "seeing." Sketch and describe any cusp-cap you see and the conditions of the observation. Try to observe Venus as close to inferior conjunction as possible—that is, close enough to see it as Morning Star and Evening Star on the same day, or close enough to see extensions of its cusps, or even close enough to see its atmosphere as a ring of light surrounding the dark planet. Be sure to sketch the planet in such observations carefully, noting directions on the drawing.

There is nothing quite like the sight of Venus as a crescent in the telescope. The crescent of Mercury (very difficult to observe) is about 6 times smaller; the crescent Moon, about 30 times bigger. Neither has more than a small fraction of the surface brightness of Venus. The drama associated with the evening crescent Venus is far different from that of the crescent Moon: Venus gets rapidly thinner but taller, gets noticeably lower and sets earlier (not later) each night, and prepares to exit and then be gone from the dusk sky for almost a year. And the last stage of that exit can offer several truly unique sights.

Even long before Venus reaches inferior conjunction, however, observers have sometimes seen a controversial sight, which, if not an optical trick, is marvelous, significant, and unique. The sight is that of a *cusp-cap*. If one point of the Venus crescent is tipped with a variation in brightness or color (or even a seeming appendage), this "cap" would usually be difficult to attribute to poor optics or poor "seeing." There is a chance that some of these caps really are observations of the area of reduced cloud-cover that is found at each of the poles of Venus.

Conjunction with the Sun means unviewability for all the planets and even the Moon, except in the cases of eclipses by the Moon and transits across the face of the Sun—cases where we see only a dark silhouette. But there is one other exception—the visibility of crescent Venus at some of its inferior conjunctions.

Even viewing Venus with the naked eye at the moment of inferior conjunction is not impossible—and not just because of the planet's brightness. The orbit of Venus is inclined somewhat to that of Earth, and, if the planets pass at the point where Venus is riding highest above the plane of Earth's orbit, then this distance in space can appear to loom as large as 9° (Venus 9° north of the Sun) in apparent distance because of Venus's closeness. The greater northerliness of Venus at such times means that observers at mid-northern latitudes can see it set a number of minutes after the Sun and rise a number of minutes before the Sun on the same day or on the morning after the evening. In fact, this situation can persist for several days around the time of inferior conjunction. (The completely opposite situation—Venus passing far south of the Sun—is favorable for observers in the Southern Hemisphere of Earth, of course.)

But it is not necessary for Venus to set a certain number of minutes after the Sun to see it on the day of inferior conjunction—perhaps even at the moment of inferior conjunction—with a telescope. One only has to have Venus enough degrees away from the Sun in the daytime sky. Telescopic observers have spotted and observed the planet when it was only 5° or 6° away from the Sun. Naturally, one must be *very* careful when looking through the telescope at an image so close to the Sun. But, however you observe Venus very near inferior conjunction, the reward can be great: the unique sight of a crescent Venus with the horns extended by sunlight shining through the Venus's atmosphere . . . even extended all the way around to make a complete circle of light!

Questions

1. Can you establish the likelihood that your sighting of a cusp-cap is not merely an effect of telescope optics or "seeing"? What does the cap look like? Can you see it again within the next few days?

2. How close to inferior conjunction can you observe Venus? Close enough to see it, at favorable apparitions, as Evening Star and Morning Star on the same day or on the opposite sides of one night? Close enough to behold cusp extensions? Close enough to see the extensions join to form a circle of light, with sunlight shining through the planet's atmosphere around its dark body?

31.

General Observations of Saturn

Observe Saturn, noting the current tilt of the rings and distinguishing at least between the brighter B ring and its outside neighbor, the A ring. Look for and sketch any detail on Saturn's globe. If the planet is anywhere near quadrature, look for the shadow of the rings on the planet and of the planet on the rings. Note the oblateness and overall color of the globe of Saturn.

The two most striking sights in a telescope for most first-time viewers are the Moon and the planet Saturn. With decent "seeing" and a properly collimated telescope (even a rather small one), the ball and rings of Saturn are beheld with a sharpness and of course a "liveness" that photos cannot convey. See Figure 17. Veteran observers would find it difficult to ever grow quite tired of this basic sight even if the presentation angle of the rings never changed (which it does, dramatically). Nevertheless, dedicated observers find an interest beyond the aesthetic enjoyment of the study in illuminated geometry or statuary of light, shadow, and shapes that is Saturn. Their goal is to observe Saturn skillfully with good telescopes in good "seeing" so as to see a wealth of possible detail beyond the basics.

In this activity, however, we deal with the basics, which are good even for the veteran planet-watcher to review or reconsider from time to time. More advanced aspects of Saturn-watching are the topics of the activities that follow.

As a superior planet (farther out from the Sun than Earth is), Saturn behaves in the sky much like Jupiter—first dawn appearance after conjunction with the Sun, west quadrature, start of retrograde motion, oppo-

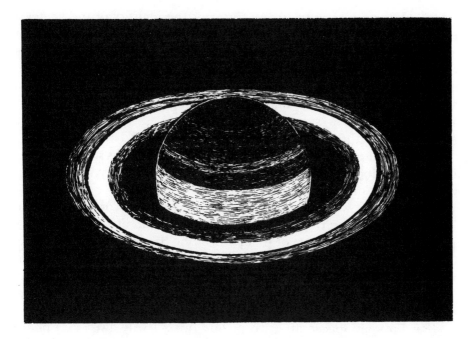

Figure 17 Saturn.

sition (rising at sunset), end of retrograde motion, east quadrature, and last dusk appearance just before conjunction with the Sun. But, Saturn is far slower than Jupiter—so slow that we can find it practical to talk about where Saturn will be and what Saturn will be doing over the course of not just a year but a whole decade.

Saturn is the slowest of the planets known to the ancients, requiring almost 30 years to complete one of its huge orbits and therefore almost 30 years to circle our entire heavens. Whereas Jupiter spends a tidy 1 year (on an average) in each zodiac constellation, Saturn is in each for an average of 2½ years and is therefore not difficult to keep track of. We can simply say, for instance, that in the 1990s Saturn will be creeping across the autumn constellations of the zodiac, itself coming to opposition in the last half of summer or first half of autumn. Saturn almost always appears as a steady, somber gold point of light of between about magnitude 0 and 1, which is comparable in brightness with a number of the brighter stars. But, since the autumn constellations contain so few bright stars, in the 1990s Saturn will tend to stand out like a solitary beacon (along with the one first-magnitude star that people at mid-northern latitudes can see in the autumn constellations, Fomalhaut).

A look through the telescope confirms the identity of the planet in spectacular fashion. Even binoculars or finderscopes can show that this image is elongated. A very small telescope and 30X or 40X magnification shows the rings as being tiny but definite. A slightly larger telescope and more magnification reveal that these are in fact rings in the plural—you may not see the thin black line that separates the two most prominent rings, the A and B rings, but the greater brightness and lightness of the inner (B ring) of the two make it stand out.

What are the rings of Saturn? Galileo's telescope was so poor that he thought they looked like "ears." About 50 years later, in the mid-seventeenth century, Christiaan Huygens was the first to see that the rings encircle the planet without touching. But it was a matter of simple physics to figure out that the rings must be composed of individual particles—stupendously large numbers of them—orbiting Saturn at whatever speed was appropriate for a given particle's distance from the planet. There could be little doubt that these particles were bits of ice, perhaps the debris of moons that came too close to Saturn and were broken or material that was too close to Saturn to have ever formed moons.

The Voyager spacecraft gave us our finest (truly awesome) photographs and other measurements of Saturn and its rings, as well as discovering or (in the case of Uranus and Neptune) helping to verify rings around all the other gas giant planets. But these other ring systems are in some ways quite different and visually paltry (none are directly visible to Earth-based telescopic observers) compared to Saturn's magnificent structures. The Voyagers revealed at Saturn seven rings (lettered A through G) but literally thousands of component "ringlets" and many peculiar ring features, including dark "spokes" on the rings. They found that some of the major divisions of the rings can be explained by the gravitational effects of various moons (Saturn now has 18 known moons), including "shepherd satellites," which can confine the particles of a thin ring between their (the satellites') orbits. But much of the structure of the rings remains unexplained.

Not only do the sky-motions of slow Saturn deserve to be discussed from the perspective of a whole decade. The telescopic view of the rings varies over a long time (although some of the changes happen in a matter of months or even weeks or days). A novice Saturn-watcher turning to look at the planet in 1995 could be shocked to find the famous, supposedly conspicuous rings as mere narrow projections from the planet—or as not even visible at all!

What happens is that the angle from which we view the rings changes. Figure 18 (which accompanies Activity 34) illustrates how the rings stay tilted at the same angle with respect to Saturn and its orbit, but the Earth's vantage-point shifts to give us anything from about a 27° to a 0° angle of the rings with respect to the horizontal. In other words, the rings can be fairly well tilted ("open"), showing us a good view across the vast expanse of their top or bottom (north face or south face), or the rings can be presented to us perfectly edge-on or "edgewise"—from a sideways view. The marvelous thing is that, although Saturn's two most prominent rings span across a distance of about 170,000 miles in the other two dimensions, their thickness is as little as a few hundred yards! The difference is tremendously greater than that between a razor-blade's width and its thickness. When Saturn's rings are exactly at edgewise, even the world's largest telescopes have difficulty distinguishing them. The next times this happens are in May of 1995, August of 1995, and February of 1996. More details on the angles of the rings, observations near edgewise, and other ring observations are discussed in Activities 34 and 35.

The rings of Saturn usually steal the show, but the globe of the planet can be very interesting, too. As with the other gas giant planets, so too with Saturn we look at only the planet's clouded atmosphere. The spacecraft passing Saturn found that it is not merely the planet's distance (somewhat less than twice that of Jupiter from the Earth) that makes its cloud features appear far fewer and subtler than those of Jupiter. The features really are far fewer and subtler. There is less activity out at much less Sun-warmed (and less internally hot) Saturn, and, most importantly, there is a layer of haze in the planet's atmosphere that greatly reduces visibility. Fortunately, there are times when features rise up through the haze so that some rare but marvelous detail is sometimes glimpsed by veteran observers (see the next activity for more details).

Even if you cannot make out any of the belts or zones of Saturn on a given night, however, there are several basic sights to look for. Two are the shadow of the planet on the rings and the shadow of the rings on the planet. These sights are best visible around the time of the quadratures, for, although Saturn itself is too similarly distant from both Earth and the Sun to really show a *phase effect* (that is, to show us any of its night side), the rings are large and elongated enough to make it possible to see some of the planet's shadow on them and some of their shadow on it.

Another aspect of Saturn's globe that is always visible, but very underappreciated, is its oblateness. This oblateness is not surprising when we consider that Saturn is the only planet with an average density much less than even that of water, and that it spins almost as rapidly as Jupiter. Saturn's diameter through its poles is about 10 percent less than through its equator—roughly one entire Earth-diameter different! The reason that even novices do not notice the oblateness more often can be laid to the account of the rings. Besides distracting us from evaluation of the planet's shape, perhaps they also lead us to subconsciously think that our perception of the planet's oblateness is an optical illusion induced by the influence of seeing the rings elongated in the planet's equatorial plane. In any case, when the rings are near edgewise and almost vanished, a look at Saturn's globe immediately shows how significantly oblate it really is.

Questions

1. What is the smallest telescope or lowest magnification with which you can detect any hint of the rings? Or see them distinctly? Or see the distinction between the brighter B ring and the A ring just outside of it?

2. What is the tilt of the rings when you observe the planet? How much is it changing over a matter of weeks or months this year?

3. Can you see any detail on Saturn's globe? Can you detect the shadow of the rings on the globe? Can you see the shadow of the planet on the rings? How easy is it for you to note the oblateness of Saturn's globe?

32.

Cloud Features of Saturn

Look for as many belts as possible on Saturn's globe. Note the color and brightness of the Equatorial Zone and whether any festoons or white spots can be glimpsed in it or elsewhere on the planet. Try judging the latitude and timing the rotation rate of any sufficiently prominent temporary feature. On nights of near-perfect "seeing," look for unusual features and for any pink in the Equatorial Zone or bluishness in the polar regions.

A medium-sized telescope that in good conditions shows many belts and zones on Jupiter will usually show just the Equatorial Zone and one or two of the belts of Saturn. And whereas small telescopes can almost always show some kind of activity—festoons, ovals, and the like—in Jupiter's clouds, glimpsing these features in Saturn's clouds is a relative rarity.

In a way, however, this paucity of Saturnian features has its advantages for the dedicated amateur observer. In the simplicity of Saturn's face, you know that almost any temporary feature that appears is worth noting carefully and even reporting. The biggest thing you need is nothing more than the patience and perseverance to keep looking.

The nomenclature for the zones and belts of Saturn is like that of Jupiter (refer back to Figure 13), but most of these features would not be visible at one time even in the best telescope. Most of them will *never* be glimpsed in the typical amateur telescope.

As with Jupiter, the equatorial belts of Saturn tend to be the most prominent. Except when the rings are near edgewise, however, only one of the equatorial belts is visible, the other one being hidden from our view by the rings. The Equatorial Zone of Saturn usually stands out well. This is partly by contrast of its yellow (or other) color to the whiter rings and partly by contrast of its brightness to whichever equatorial belt is being seen. Apparently, however, it also really is brighter and more colorful than the other (seldom distinguishable) zones of the planet.

Faint festoons sometimes extend into the Equatorial Zone from an equatorial belt, and, very infrequently, white spots may be observed. The spots are generally very subtle features, and such features are small enough on distant Saturn to require something on the order of at least 250X magnification to see properly.

Whenever a reasonably prominent spot or festoon is observed, the observer should try to time how long it takes to rotate around the planet (with Saturn's lack of visible belts and zones to use as references, you may need to make your estimate of a feature's latitude very carefully). Unlike Jupiter, which has its rotation rates divided fairly accurately into System I and II rates that are only about 5 minutes different, Saturn has System I and II rotations that differ by about 24 minutes. Also unlike Jupiter, Saturn has a System II that is only an approximation for what seems to be a considerable range of different rates, slowing with increasing latitude. System I on Saturn applies to the features of the Equatorial Zone and the two equatorial belts on either side of it. The System I rotation rate is about 10 hours, 14 minutes. System II rotation applies to the rest of Saturn, but the figure is only an average of 10 hours, 38 minutes.

To improve the visibility of features on Saturn, a yellow filter may be found useful—that is, when there are features to see.

Rarely, there are sensational features to see. The white spots of Saturn are usually subtle, but, at least once in each revolution of Saturn— apparently at roughly the same place in its orbit—the planet seems to break out with a Great White Spot. The most recent outbreak, which occurred in the autumn of 1990, proved to be a mighty one, comparable with (or even more dramatic than?) the great one of 1933. In both cases, the feature apparently first appeared as a brilliant, very white, roundish patch in the Equatorial Zone and rapidly elongated so that in a few weeks most of the planet was encircled. The brightness and whiteness of the Great White Spot are remarkable. Visible in small telescopes, the Spot is comparable (as more than one of us independently thought in 1990) to the reflectivity and color of a Martian polar cap.

The Great White Spot must be a disturbance that brings up warmer ammonia gas powerfully high into Saturn's atmosphere, where it freezes to produce brilliant, white clouds of ammonia ice crystals.

The Great White Spot of 1990 may linger with related patchy activity well into 1991 but probably no longer. And it will probably not recur for roughly another 30 years. But you can never tell—might a second outbreak of the Spot occur in the near future, before the planet has moved much farther along its orbit?

Although a recurrence of the Great White Spot may not happen anytime soon, Saturn is noted for sometimes giving its observers remarkable detail on a night of near-perfect "seeing" when there is activity going on in its clouds. And colors other than the usual yellow may sometimes be seen—a salmon pink in the Equatorial Zone or a distinct bluishness in the polar regions. Such details will take not only excellent "seeing" but also perhaps a telescope at least in the 10- to 12-inch range as well as many, many nights of looking unsuccessfully for them. But, for such views of a planet like Saturn, the wait and the work are easily worth it.

Questions

1. What belts can you see on Saturn tonight? Is the Equatorial Zone distinctly brighter than the planet's other light areas?

2. Can you see any sign of other features, like festoons or white spots? If so, can you estimate their latitudes as accurately as possible and time their rotation rates around the planet?

3. If you see any outburst comparable to the Great White Spot, can you sketch it carefully each night that it is visible to chronicle its development?

4. What very rare features and colors can you see on Saturn with a large telescope under near-perfect "seeing" conditions? Do you note any pink in the Equatorial Zone? Any bluish hue in the polar caps?

33.

The Rings of Saturn and Their Features

Note the difference in brightness and color between the A ring and the B ring of Saturn, and study Cassini's division between them. Look for Encke's division in the A ring and any other divisions you might notice, taking great care to sketch their positions accurately. Look for the C, or Crepe, ring, estimating its visibility, its width in comparison to the B ring, and the appearance of any gap between it and the B ring. Look for differences in the prominence of a division, or of any intensification, as seen in one ansa of the rings compared to the other. Search for the presence of any Terby Spots on the B ring.

The rings of Saturn are the most famous special planetary feature in the solar system and, in most people's opinion, the most beautiful such feature.

Unlike most of the other famous features (like the Great Red Spot), the rings are spectacularly easy to see in even a very small telescope. They are large: Saturn is almost twice as far as Jupiter but the main ring system's span is almost twice as great as Jupiter's width and thus appears roughly as wide (sometimes considerably wider). They are bright: When they are fairly open (considerably tilted), they reflect more total light to us than the ball of the planet, and in some years their changing angle creates quite noticeable changes in Saturn's naked-eye brightness. They are sharp: This is especially noticeable in comparison to the globes of planets like Jupiter and Saturn, where the limb is fuzzy and dimmer due to the absorption of light along a longer, grazing pathway of very cloudy, deep atmosphere. And, of course, the rings offer an alternative—as well as a splendid accompaniment—to the form of the sphere in planetary observation.

The rings also offer variety. One kind of variety is in the changing angle with which they are presented to us. This is discussed as part of our next two activities. The present activity is devoted to the exciting variety of the components and features that can be seen when the ring system is well tilted. Three major rings and at least two ring divisions are within reasonable reach of amateur telescopes.

Even a small telescope shows that the outermost major visible ring, the A ring, is not as bright or light-colored as the next ring inward, the B ring. You can help keep straight in your mind which letter applies to which ring by remembering that the B ring is the brightest and broadest (both adjectives begin with the letter "B").

The narrow gap between the A and B rings will not be seen with very small telescopes or even by somewhat larger ones when the rings start to get very close to edgewise. Given a night of good "seeing," a decent 4-inch (or even slightly smaller) telescope, and the rings fairly open, however, you should be able to detect as a narrow black line the gap known as *Cassini's division*. As you observe it, consider that this narrow division is actually about as wide as Earth's Atlantic Ocean! This gives you a better idea of the immensity of the rings.

One of numerous interesting findings by the Voyager spacecraft was the confirmation that Cassini's division and other divisions are not completely empty of ring particles. An unusual chance for earthbound astronomers to see this (at least indirectly) for themselves occurred in 1988, when a fairly bright star could be observed passing behind the rings and shining through them. The brightness of the star varied, even within the major divisions, proving that at least some obscuring bodies must be present.

While Cassini's division is the most dependable and prominent, another that may sometimes be glimpsed in medium-to-large telescopes is *Encke's division*. Encke's division does not separate two major rings; it is a gap within the A ring. In 1990, scientists confirmed that an eighteenth moon of Saturn actually orbits within Encke's division. The visibility of Encke's division seems to be somewhat variable, and this is also true for a number of other divisions in the rings that amateurs may hope to glimpse from time to time. The variability really does seem to reside in the rings themselves, and thus sketching the position of these divisions on the infrequent occasions when you see them could provide some important information for scientists. Remember that study of the Voyager data has not yet enabled scientists to be certain what creates most of the ring divisions. Any observations that could help show how the ring structures have changed since the Voyager flybys could be very illuminating. Of course, such observations are likely to be made only by the careful observer who has put in many, many nights at the telescope with Saturn.

A third ring of Saturn is sometimes not too difficult to glimpse with medium-sized telescopes. This is the innermost visible ring, the C ring, or Crepe ring. This ring is far thinner and more transparent than the others and suffers from having both the bright B ring and globe of the planet near it. The most interesting thing about it is how variable its visibility is. Once again, as with the ring divisions, this variability almost certainly does reside in the ring itself; it is almost certainly not just a product of the observing conditions on Earth. The Crepe ring is sometimes difficult to see in the largest telescopes; at other times, it is quite detectable in a 6-inch telescope. It is presumably losing and gaining particles in various ways at various times. A study of its variability is a good project for amateur astronomers. Besides estimating its prominence, try to judge also how wide it appears in relation to the B ring and whether you can detect any gap between it and the B ring. Be sure to make careful notes about sky transparency and "seeing," of course.

There are other peculiar features in the rings that might be spied by skillful observers under excellent conditions. Sketches of Saturn made before the Pioneer and Voyager flybys (some made with very large and others with not so large telescopes) show a profusion of detail. Some of this detail was confirmed by Voyager. One now-famous example was eagle-eyed *Sky & Telescope* editor Steve O'Meara's sightings of the strange "spokes" (dark radial markings on the rings) before the spacecraft revealed them to us all. Such observations demonstrate that, more than perhaps any planet, Saturn offers the potential for glimpsing a tremendous number of additional exquisite and scientifically important details if the observer, the telescope, and the night are all excellent.

Look for any variations in the rings' brightness; if there can be gaps of varying prominence, there should also be intensifications of varying prominence. Whenever you see a division or intensification in one part of Saturn's rings, look to see whether it is matched on the opposite end of the rings by a similarly prominent division or intensification. Often, observers find that it is not; one ansa looks different from the other. The term *ansa*—plural, *ansae*—refers to the parts of the rings to either side of the planet, the areas of apparently greatest curvature.

The spokes have not really been satisfactorily explained yet, but I wonder if they are not related to a less rarely glimpsed sight—large, very bright, oval patches on the B ring called *Terby Spots*.

Questions

1. How small of a telescope and how large of a magnification are needed to see Cassini's division under various conditions (including various tilts of the rings)? What telescope and magnification suffice to show the distinction between the brightness and color of the A and B rings?

2. Can you detect Encke's division or any of the other usually more difficult-to-see ring divisions? Are there any differences in the promi-

nence of such divisions (or any intensifications in the rings) that are seen in one ansa as compared to those seen (or not seen!) in the other?

3. Can you detect the C, or Crepe, ring? If so, how prominent is it with different telescopes under different conditions? How much does its prominence vary as seen with the same telescope under similar conditions? How much does its width and the presence of any gap between it and the B ring vary?

4. Can you see any variations in brightness in a particular ring? Can you detect and carefully sketch any Terby Spots on the B ring?

34.

Saturn's Rings Near Edgewise—Part 1

As the angle of tilt of Saturn's rings decreases, note when you can no longer detect various features or aspects of the rings, such as Cassini's division, the distinction in color and brightness between the A ring and the B ring, and so on. Draw the appropriate outline of the rings for each change in its form, and sketch carefully what is visible. When the rings get near edgewise, sketch the different levels of brightness in different parts of them and where these occur. Look for transits, shadow transits, eclipses, and occultations of Saturn's moons that are not visible at other times. When the rings are very near edgewise, note the position of clumps or beads of light on them (caused by actual thicker areas of ring particles), making sure to distinguish these from the transiting moons (whose positions you can look up in the Astronomical Almanac*).*

A further kind of variety of Saturn's rings is their changing angle of presentation to us. When the rings are most open, they are tilted over 26° from the horizontal toward us; when the rings are edgewise, they are tilted 0° from the horizontal toward us. Figure 18 explains why these appearances occur. The edgewise presentations happen only around the two

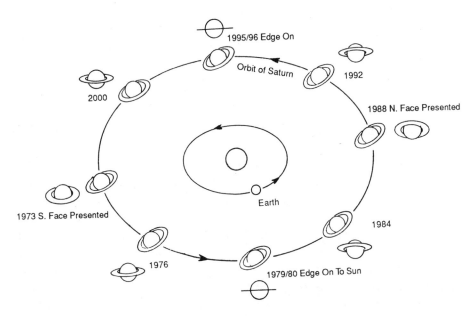

Figure 18 Saturn's Orbit and Explanation of the Rings' Tilt. View of Saturn is inverted, as in a telescope.

places in Saturn's 29.5-year orbit where the plane of Earth's orbit crosses the plane of the ring system.

Marvels are seen at the times of these presentations because of an amazing fact: The rings are roughly a million times thinner than they are wide or broad! These glorious structures, normally visible in almost the smallest telescopes, may vanish without a trace in even the world's largest telescopes when they are presented to Earth edgewise! A span of rings that could cover most of the distance between Earth and Moon, dwarfing both, is reduced to a line of light a city block or two wide—seemingly nothing, because finally too narrow to see from over three-quarters of a billion miles away.

The periods between the times of edgewiseness are alternately 15.75 years and 13.75 years. In the former period, the tops of the rings (the northern part) are presented to us; in the latter period, the bottoms of the rings (the southern part) are presented to us. The reason for the difference in the length of the two periods involves when Saturn reaches *perihelion* (closest to the Sun in space) and when Saturn reaches *aphelion* (farthest from the Sun in space). The half of its orbit that contains its perihelion point is the half on which Saturn moves faster. Presumably by coincidence,

109

the time when the rings are most open is near to the times of perihelion and aphelion. For instance, Saturn's rings were most open in 1973, and perihelion occurred in 1974; Saturn's rings were most open in 1987, and aphelion occurred in 1988.

If the rings were not most open near the time of aphelion, the planet's point of light would then be much dimmer. In fact, for a few years around the time of their being most open, the rings are actually reflecting to us more light than the planet itself. With the rings open, the planet approaches magnitude 0 around opposition. With the rings at edgewise, the planet is almost a whole magnitude fainter (it is as dim as magnitude 1.5 if the planet is then far from opposition). If Earth and the Sun could ever see the rings face-on, distant Saturn would rival the brightness of Jupiter in our sky.

The most important fact about the periods between edgewise presentations for observers is not, of course, that they alternate between different lengths of time. It is that these periods are so long. If the rings are near edgewise now, you have a long wait before they are again most open; likewise, if the rings are most open, you have a long wait until the next time you can see the strange sights around the time of edgewiseness. Table 5 reveals more information. It gives the angle and date when the rings are most open and least open each year over the period from 1987 through 1999. The yearly fluctuation (more open, then less open, then more open) is largely due to Earth's position in its orbit. Notice that, for years when the rings are the most open of all (near a maximum tilt of almost 27°), the angle of tilt stays fairly near the maximum and does not vary greatly during the course of a year. But, as the rings approach edgewise presentation, the angle becomes more sensitive to Earth's position and fluctuates drastically.

As the rings un-tilt toward edgewiseness, there are many consequences for observers. The outline of the rings on which you will sketch details in your drawings will have to change as the tilt decreases. It is difficult to keep track of exactly what the outline will be, especially during the radical fluctuations in the years nearest to edgewiseness. Table 5 also gives figures at oppositions from 1987 to 1999 for the minor axis of the rings in millimeters if the major axis is set at 100 mm. As you can see, at the oppositions nearest to the time of most-openness (the latter—most-open—last occurred in November of 1987), the minor axis is almost half as great as the major. The outer edge of the visible rings then sticks out a little beyond the top and the bottom of the planet.

Near edgewiseness, feature after feature of the rings that we have been accustomed to viewing disappear—all the more subtle divisions and features, then Cassini's division, then even the distinction between the major rings—as all fold up into a single line of light. In compensation, marvelous new observations become possible: only around edgewiseness can the more inner satellites of Saturn be glimpsed; only around then can Saturnian satellites be seen to transit and have their shadows transit Saturn, get eclipsed and occulted by Saturn. The rings themselves provide startling new opportunities for us to learn things about them around edgewiseness.

Table 5
Angle of Saturn's Ring-Tilt and Proportion of Rings' Major to Minor Axis, 1987–1999*

Year	Opp. Date§	Minor Axis**	Max. Tilt & Max. Date§§		Min. Tilt & Min. Date***	
1987	Jun 9	44 mm	26.56°	Jan 29	26.44°	May 14
			26.89°	Nov 23		
1988	Jun 20	45 mm	26.93°	Sep 24	26.12°	Apr 14
1989	Jul 2	42 mm	26.12°	Sep 19	24.68°	Apr 22
1990	Jul 14	38 mm	24.25°	Sep 26	22.23°	May 2
1991	Jul 26	35 mm	21.38°	Oct 5	18.86°	May 14
1992	Aug 7	31 mm	17.64°	Oct 15	14.77°	May 24
1993	Aug 19	25 mm	13.17°	Oct 26	10.04°	Jun 6
1994	Sep 1	12 mm§§§	8.13°	Nov 6	4.86°	Jun 18
1995	Sep 14	0 mm§§§	0.62°	Jul 1	0.00°	May 21
			2.67°	Nov 18	0.00°	Aug 11
1996	Sep 26	9 mm§§§	6.20°	Jul 13	0.00°	Feb 11
					3.20°	Nov 29
1997	Oct 10	16 mm§§§	11.66°	Jul 26	8.72°	Dec 11
1998	Oct 23	26 mm	16.72°	Aug 9	14.19°	Dec 23
1999	Nov 6	35 mm	21.06°	Aug 22	19.09°	1/4/2000

* Figures for minor axis derived from James Muirden, *How to Use an Astronomical Telescope*; figures for ring-tilts and ring-tilt dates calculated by Steve Albers (personal communication).

§ Opposition date.

** Size of the minor axis of the ring outline if the major axis is drawn as 100 mm.

§§ Maximum tilt of rings and date it occurs (twice in some years).

*** Minimum tilt of rings and date it occurs (twice in some years).

§§§ Approximate size.

With good "seeing" and with medium-to-large telescopes, observers will often notice that the nearly edgewise line of the rings is brighter in some parts than in others. The different levels of brightness should be estimated on a 1-to-10 scale, and the positions of the different areas depicted as accurately as possible on sketches. When the rings get really close to being presented edge-on, the brighter areas will seem to show themselves for what they are—thicker regions of ring particles—by appearing as clumps or beads of light on the narrow line of the rings. But it is important not to confuse this phenomenon with another marvelous one, the sight of the Saturnian satellites appearing like "beads" moving along the "thread" of the rings. You must check the positions of the satellites given in the *Astronomical Almanac*—or in one of the popular astronomy magazines, for surely they will be giving intense coverage to the upcoming 1995–1996 series of edgewise presentations.

Series? Yes, the variety of Saturn's ring appearances is masterfully and beautifully increased still further by the fact that edgewise presentations are often not single events separated by those 13.75- and 15.75-year periods. Our next activity continues with discussion of what happens during these series and with different observational chances made possible by the Sun's positioning with respect to the rings.

Questions

1. At what ring-tilt angle (measured in degrees from edgewiseness, the horizontal), can you last detect the lesser-known divisions of the rings? Encke's division? Cassini's division? The A ring and the B ring as distinct entities made different from each other by their brightness and color?

2. What rare transits and shadow transits, eclipses, and occultations of Saturn's moons can you see when the rings are fairly near edgewise?

3. What clumps or beads of light caused by thicker areas of ring particles can you detect and carefully sketch the position of as the rings get very near edgewise? Are you sure that these beads are not moons of Saturn transiting? (Check the moons' positions in the *Astronomical Almanac* or elsewhere.)

35.

Saturn's Rings Near Edgewise—Part 2

Observe the rings in each of the following situations: (1) passing through edgewise into darkness; (2) passing through edgewise back into sunlight; (3) passing, while still tilted a bit toward Earth, into darkness; and (4) passing through edgewise back into sunlight a second time. During the periods when we see the night side of the rings, look for gleams of light leaking through and sketch their positions accurately. Observe the rings as near to the time of edgewise as possible and with as many telescopes as possible.

After waiting 13.75 or 15.75 years to see Saturn's rings edgewise again, we find that most edgewise presentations come in a series of three.

In most cases, the positions of Earth and Saturn are such that our orbit's inclination with respect to that of the ring-plane allows us to go through the ring-plane several times within a roughly 9-month period—to bob below, above, and below (as in 1995–1996) or above, below, and above the ring-plane (as in 1979–1980). In such cases, the middle event tends to occur near opposition (very favorably placed); the others, far enough from conjunction with the Sun. But there are times when only one ring-plane passage occurs, and that quite near conjunction. This is what will happen in both 2009 and 2025. So it is crucial for observers to study well and enjoy thoroughly the upcoming series of edgewise presentations in 1995–1996—there will not be another chance to see a series or to see an edgewise presentation high in a midnight sky after that for over 40 years! (The astronomy magazines should indeed pull out all the stops to give us thorough treatment of this last opportunity in 1995–1996.)

There is one further fascinating complication of the edgewise presentations. And that is the matter of which part, top or bottom (north or south), of the rings is being illuminated by the Sun. There is only one passage of the Sun through the ring-plane, and it can occur either a little while before or a little while after a single-event passage of Earth through the ring-plane. The passage of the Sun occurs *during* the 9-month time that spans a series of three passages of Earth through the ring-plane, but exactly when it occurs will determine when various observations are possible. The observations of bright clumpings in the near-edgewise rings will not be possible during a period when the Sun is shining on the north face of the rings if it is the southern face that is tilted slightly toward Earth, or vice versa. You might say that such a period is the only time we get to see the night side of the rings. The dark line of them must then be distinguished from their narrow shadow nearby. But, remember, the rings are far from opaque. Now the great challenge will be to detect where bits of light leak through them and to record the positions accurately on your sketches. To clarify what the various passages of Earth and the Sun through the ring-plane mean for observers, a chronology of the 1995–1996 events follows:

May 21, 1995. Earth passes from north to south of ring-plane. Rings are presented edgewise; then dark side of them is presented. (This is about 2½ months after conjunction with Sun, so planet is fairly high in dawn sky.)

August 11, 1995. Earth passes from south to north of ring-plane. Rings are presented edgewise; then sunlit side bursts into view. (This is about 1 month before opposition, so planet rises in early evening and is very high in sky in middle of night.)

November 19, 1995. Sun passes from north to south of ring-plane. Rings are not presented edgewise; they are suddenly cast into darkness again, with only occasional leaks of light slipping through them. (This is about 2 months after opposition, so planet gets very high in evening sky.)

February 11, 1996. Earth passes from north to south of ring-plane again. Rings are presented edgewise, then burst into sunlight and become more tilted. (This is about 1 month before conjunction with Sun, so planet appears rather low in dusk sky.)

How close to the moment of edgewiseness can you still detect the rings in telescopes of various sizes? If the night side of the rings is presented, they will become invisible days or even weeks before edgewiseness. But, if the sunlit side is presented, a 6-inch telescope might reveal the needle-thin rings up to about a day or so before edgewiseness; larger telescopes, up until even hours before.

Questions

1. What sights can you sketch at each stage in the passages of Saturn's rings through edgewise to Earth and to the Sun? Can you detect gleams of sunlight shining through the rings when their night side is presented?

2. How soon before and after each edgewise presentation of the rings can you detect them in telescopes of various sizes?

36.

The Satellites of Saturn

Locate and view as many of Saturn's moons as you can with telescopes of different sizes. Observe Titan frequently, each time trying to make an estimate of its color. Follow the brightness variation of Iapetus from its western to eastern elongation and back again. Observe each of the Saturnian moons individually while pondering its physical nature as revealed by the Voyagers. When Saturn is near edgewise, try to observe eclipses, occultations, transits, and shadow transits of the moons, especially of Titan. Note how much easier it is to see the inner moons, especially difficult Mimas, at each stage as the rings get closer to edgewise.

We know (see Activities 23 and 24) that four of Jupiter's moons are huge, easily visible, and constantly busy in eclipses, occultations, and other events. Only one of Saturn's moons is truly huge, and neither it nor any of the other visible Saturnian satellites pass in front of or behind the planet except during certain periods that are many years apart.

But what Saturn's moons lack in size and involvement in eclipses, they make up for in number. Jupiter has a total of at least 16 moons, of which only the four biggest are easily identifiable in telescopes. Saturn has a total of at least 18 moons, of which six can be glimpsed in a 6- or 8-inch telescope in dark skies. A somewhat larger telescope can reveal two more moons. See Figure 19.

The Voyager spacecraft showed that the Saturnian satellite system is remarkably complex and something more—replete with glorious wreckage. The rings may be largely material that came too close to the planet to form into moons, but many Saturnian moons show the signs of having been devastated by collisions or other violent events. The moon Mimas has a crater more than one-quarter the diameter of the moon itself. Two other moons come incredibly close to each other before switching orbits and are thought to be the halves of what was once a single satellite. The moon Hyperion is rather big but is shaped like a hamburger, and it is still reeling so much from some past violence that it has chaotic rotation—every rotation period from no rotation to many hours, every cardinal direction changing. There are several cases of two or three Saturnian moons following one another around in the same orbit.

There are many other strange cases among the moons of Saturn. The most recent discovery of a Saturnian satellite came in 1990 when exhaus-

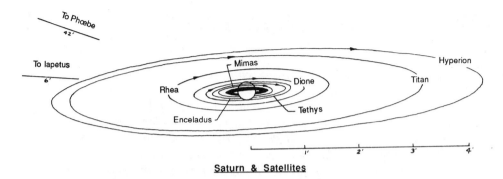

Figure 19 Orbits of Observable Saturnian Satellites. The apparent shapes of the orbits change as seen from Earth during the course of the Saturnian year. This view is only roughly what the orientation is in the early 1990s.

tive study of Voyager images revealed a tiny moon about 12 miles (20 km) across orbiting within the A ring's Encke's division, which is about 200 miles (325 km) wide.

Mimas and Hyperion are the most difficult to see of the eight moons of Saturn within range of amateur telescopes. The other moons previously mentioned are mostly too dim, although among the satellites that share their orbit with other (little) ones are fairly large, fairly bright Tethys and Dione. Then there is Iapetus. This moon varies in brightness by about 2 magnitudes from one side of its orbit to the other because of a strange covering of one part of its surface. This dark substance may be derived from the one satellite in the system more distant from Saturn than Iapetus—backward-orbiting Phoebe.

Table 6 lists the eight visible satellites in order of distance from the planet, with their orbital periods and their magnitudes at a typical opposition. The order of their visibility is roughly as follows: Titan, Iapetus at its brightest, Rhea, Dione, Tethys, Iapetus at its dimmest, Enceladus, Hyperion, and Mimas. The popular astronomy magazines always carry information on where the major moons will be for a month or two around the time of opposition; several annual publications give the positions for the whole year. What follows here are notes about the moons in order of visibility, giving several of the special observations of them that can be tried. But, of course, the challenge of finding as many of them as possible on a given night with a given telescope is itself a fascinating project.

1. Titan is the second largest moon of the solar system. It is not much smaller than Ganymede and is considerably larger than the

116

Table 6
Observable Satellites of Saturn*

	Magnitude§	Orbital Period**
Mimas	13.1	0.9424
Enceladus	11.9	1.370
Tethys	10.4	1.888
Dione	10.6	2.737
Rhea	9.9	4.518
Titan	8.5	15.95
Hyperion	14.4	21.28
Iapetus	10–12	79.33

* Data derived from *Sky & Telescope.*
§ Magnitude at a fairly typical opposition.
** Orbital period in sidereal days.

planet Mercury. It is a moon with an atmosphere denser than that of Earth. Its clouds and haze prevented even a close passage of it by Voyager 1 from revealing the surface. Voyager did discover additional chemicals in spectra from Titan, making still more complex the speculations about conditions on the surface and how much they resemble those on the ancient Earth. Titan is an 8th magnitude object as seen from Earth. It is an easy binocular sight when it is out near its greatest elongations of about 3 arc-minutes from Saturn. Voyager showed its color to be orange, and earthbound observers have noted this color. One source I have consulted, however, says that Titan's color varies and has appeared white, yellowish, pink, or even red due to the organic compounds in its nitrogen atmosphere. Make a regular program of observing Titan and noting its color to see what you can ascertain. When Titan transits Saturn, it is said to appear almost as dark as its shadow.

2. Iapetus is 10th magnitude at its western elongations, 12th magnitude at its eastern (for the reason just discussed). This moon ranges out about 9 to 10 arc-minutes from Saturn.

3. Rhea is 10th magnitude and gets not much more than a minute of arc out from Saturn. It is the second largest of Saturn's satellites, a little wider than Iapetus, but only about half the width of Earth's Moon.

4. Dione is a bit dimmer than Rhea and a little closer to Saturn.

Even at greatest elongation, it is no more than about one span of the rings away from the planet.

5. Tethys is similar in brightness to Rhea but is a bit nearer to Saturn.

6. Enceladus is not much closer to Saturn than Tethys but shines about 1½ magnitudes dimmer than Tethys and is thus significantly harder to see.

7. Hyperion is 14th magnitude but is a little more distant from Saturn than Titan. It can thus be spotted in a 10- or 12-inch (may be smaller) telescope under excellent conditions—if you know exactly where to look.

8. Mimas is 13th magnitude but never appears more than about a single width of the combined A and B rings away from the outer edge of the A ring. Thus, it is difficult to see in even large amateur telescopes. The time when it becomes far easier to see is, of course, when the rings are near edgewise. At such times, a few expert amateurs with large telescopes have the possibility of seeing one of the dimmer moons even closer to Saturn.

Questions

1. How many moons of Saturn can you observe with telescopes of various sizes? How far out from the planet does an inner moon have to be before you can spot it?

2. What do you judge is the color of Titan? Does this color change over a short or long period of time? If so, do you find that the changes seem to be independent of observing conditions?

3. What is the physical nature and any peculiarities of each of the Saturnian satellites you observe?

4. Can you spot difficult Hyperion and even more difficult Mimas? How much does the difficulty of seeing Mimas and other inner moons decrease as the rings get closer and closer to edgewise?

37.

General Observations of Mars

Follow Mars during the course of one of its apparitions or at least during whatever stages come after the time you start your observing program. If you can commence at the beginning of an apparition, observe Mars as a disk as tiny as Uranus low in the east before dawn. Later, note when you can first see any feature on the planet. Around the time of west quadrature, examine the striking phase effect of Mars and intensify your observations of whatever dark markings or polar cap you can see. Around opposition, make intensive observations of the surface features and atmospheric features (refer to Activities 39 through 42 for advice once you have done some trial observations and sketching). Follow Mars through the above stages in reverse order, noting the differences caused by further progress of the Martian season, until Mars is lost in the dusk at apparition's end.

The most fascinating of worlds beyond our own is the planet Mars. It is the planet most like Earth, though also shockingly, beautifully, and enlighteningly different. No other planet holds promise of hosting large colonies of human beings in the next 25 to 50 years. Mars is earthlike enough to make its colonization seem almost inevitable if the political climate on Earth does not worsen horribly. And an international mission to Mars might do much to improve that climate—the planet named for the god of war helping to foster peace on Earth.

For naked-eye observers, Mars is the planet with the most distinctive color—a golden orange so impressive that it has inspired us to call Mars "the Red Planet." For telescopic observers, Mars is often said to be the only planet that shows surface features. While Venus, Jupiter, and the planets beyond Jupiter are indeed always cloud-enshrouded, this statement overlooks the possibility of seeing some surface features on elusive Mercury. There is no doubt, however, that Mars can display far more and far sharper markings than Mercury.

The only catchword here is "can." More than any other planet that can ever provide an excellent detailed view, Mars is able to remain unviewable near the Sun for a long time and, even when visible, to appear tiny and blank in the telescope for a very long time. In fact, the periods when it swells large enough to have an astonishing wealth of details proliferate on its disk occur only at very infrequent intervals and only at certain of its oppositions. But the remarkable difference between various apparitions of Mars is a topic for our next activity. In the present activity, let's follow Mars through an "average" apparition— one in which it comes neither extremely close to us nor misses us by an extremely great distance at opposition—one much like the Mars apparition of 1992–1993, in fact.

Mars orbits at about 1½ times as far as Earth from the Sun, taking almost twice as long as Earth to complete an orbit. This means that it requires about 780 days for Earth to catch up to Mars a second time, or about 780 days between one opposition of Mars and the next. This synodic period is far larger than that of any other planet and determines the way Mars tends to be in telescopes, far and small for one year, close and large the next. An apparition of Mars lasts far longer than that of any other planet, as does its period of unviewability near the Sun between apparitions.

As with any superior planet, an apparition of Mars begins with its first sighting low in the morning twilight after conjunction with the Sun. The reason why the sighting occurs many weeks after conjunction, compared to just a few weeks for Jupiter and Saturn, is twofold. First of all, Mars on the far side of its orbit from us appears decidedly dimmer than Saturn and tremendously dimmer than Jupiter. Thus, the Red Planet does not get glimpsed until it gets somewhat higher, out of the glow of the brighter twilight. The second reason for the delay in the sighting is the eastward orbital speed of Mars, which is so much greater than that of the other superior planets.

When Mars does begin to get reasonably high in a dark sky before dawn, we can notice how it keeps almost the same altitude week after week while the constellations are carried far more rapidly westward by Earth's own (eastward) motion in orbit around the Sun. It is like Mars is the actor, coming to the same spot in the sky at the same time each morning but having the background scenery (the constellations) roll on by as the weeks pass. The brightness of Mars is only about second magnitude at this stage, and consequently many a novice may have trouble spotting it among what may be as many as a dozen or so stars as bright or brighter in this general section of the heavens. (Mars has tricked a number of observers who lost track of its whereabouts into thinking it was a new exploding star, or "nova," here in the pre-dawn sky!)

When you do get your telescope on the correct second-magnitude object and see a planetary disk, you may be shocked to discover it is only about 3½ arc-seconds in width. Mars can appear slightly smaller in the telescope than Uranus, a planet almost 2 billion miles away! You will notice the ocher color of the disk but no features.

When Mars is about 60° from the Sun, its disk has grown to about 6 arc-seconds, the minimum size at which even the people who are the ALPO Mars Recorders feel that "useful" observations of the planet may be possible. Find out whether your telescope and level of experience turn up any features on Mars at this stage on nights of good "seeing."

Mars reaches western quadrature, 90° west of the Sun. It is at its highest around dawn and shows a remarkably wide shadowed edge from *phase effect* (the earthward and sunward faces of Mars can be different enough around this time to show us quite a bit of the night side of Mars).

By this stage, Mars has improved to roughly magnitude 0 and 10 arc-seconds across. Good medium-sized telescopes now begin to show a few features to the careful observer under good "seeing" conditions. A few of Mars's darker markings (gray in small telescopes, a bit green in large telescopes) can be sighted. The most prominent is often the triangular Syrtis Major, located not far north of the Martian equator. It is difficult to miss at this stage if it is near the central meridian of Mars, facing Earth, at the hour you are looking. A white glint of a polar ice cap is also likely to be spotted. The appearance of even these most prominent of Martian features is, however, greatly dependent on the current seasonal conditions on Mars. Some of the seasonal effects, such as the melting of polar ice caps, can be predicted fairly well in general. Others, like the famous dust storms of Mars, are more irregular in occurrence and varying in scope so that no one can be sure of when or even whether they will appear. Once in a while, a planetwide dust storm can hide all the Martian features (and make Mars appear slightly brighter) for many weeks. Thus, you can never tell just what you will see when you gaze through a telescope at this surprising world.

Because Mars is so much closer to Earth than Jupiter or Saturn is, its retrograde loop as Earth begins to overtake it is larger, but begins later (closer to opposition) and lasts for a shorter time. When you see the Red Planet halt and start to go westward with respect to the background stars, you know that opposition is only about a month away.

An average opposition of Mars has the planet rivaling or surpassing the brightness of the brightest star (Sirius at magnitude -1.5) and swelling to about 15 arc-seconds in width, or about 5 times Mars's apparent width when it is near conjunction. This is just about the threshold at which the few details on the planet begin to proliferate into numerous features in medium-sized telescopes. In the activities that follow, we will discuss the specifics of what can then be viewed on the Martian surface and in the Martian atmosphere, as well as how these observations are best carried out.

After opposition, Mars goes through the stages just described in reverse order and in the evening sky. It will never look the same, however, because of the inevitable seasonal changes going on. Finally, like a swimmer battling upstream (eastward) as the current (the constellations) sweeps past, but slowly being carried back (westward), Mars is ever so slowly lost in the after-sunset glow.

Questions

1. How soon after its conjunction with the Sun can you spot Mars? Can you see it when its apparent size is smaller than that of incredibly distant Uranus? How many months after conjunction do you first notice any feature on Mars?

2. When can you first detect a phase effect on Mars? How large do your drawings show this phase effect to be around western quadrature? When do you first see a polar ice cap or polar cloud hood? How many dark markings are visible on Mars on the best nights at this stage?

3. How many features (dark markings, yellow dust clouds, white polar ice, white ice clouds) do you see in your initial looks at the planet around opposition?

4. What differences in the appearances of Martian features do you note as it recedes in the evening sky compared to those at the same stages in its approach in the morning sky?

38.

The Different Kinds of Apparitions of Mars

During each apparition, and around the time of each opposition, of Mars, note which surface markings become visible at which time and at which Mars diameter. Note also the differences in how the planet is tilted toward us at each opposition, as well as the differences in both the expected and the unpredicted seasonal effects in each opposition (partly as a function of the distance of Mars from the Sun). At perihelic or very close oppositions, look for the largest topographic features on Mars (see Activity 40 for details) and for the moons of Mars.

In ancient times, many cultures associated the planet we now call Mars with their god of war or disaster. No doubt the color—which reminded the superstitious of blood—contributed to this identification. But perhaps more important was the rapid and great brightenings of Mars as it approached opposition. You might think that because an opposition of Mars occurred about every 2 years, it could become familiar. But what must have really frightened the superstitious was the way that some oppositions of Mars are much brighter than others—and one, just one every 15 or 17 years, is spectacularly brighter.

We know now that the explanation for the differences in oppositions of Mars is merely a matter of some interesting orbital geometry. But we can still find ourselves awed by the great oppositions of Mars—and keep careful track of how the current opposition we observe fits into the progress of increasingly good or increasingly poor ones in the cycle leading up to or away from the perihelic one.

The reason that oppositions of Mars differ so greatly lies in the ellipticity of Mars's orbit.

Whereas Earth's orbit is almost circular, Mars's orbit deviates significantly from this form. See Figure 20. There is a 17-percent difference between the distance of Mars at *perihelion* (closest to the Sun in space) and *aphelion* (farthest from the Sun in space). If Mars comes to opposition when it is near aphelion, the planet does not get very close to Earth (in fact, Mercury can be closer to Earth at such times). If Mars comes to opposition when it is near perihelion (perihelic opposition), it can be almost twice as close, or less than 36 million miles from Earth. Only Venus can approach Earth closer than this, but Venus does so showing almost all night side and lying too near our line of sight with the Sun to see easily. When Mars comes closest, its disk is fully lit, shining bright all night long, and highest in the midnight sky.

A word about the brightness of Mars. Of all the planets (if we do not count transits of Venus), really only Mercury can vary about as much in brightness or, very rarely, more in brightness. But Mercury's range of variation is not ever even close to being fully visible (the planet, when brightest and especially when faintest, is very near the Sun in the sky). The great change in the brightness of Mars is visible high in the midst of the night. Even during an apparition leading to an aphelic opposition, Mars will get about 3 magnitudes (about 16 times) brighter. But during a perihelic opposition, the change approaches 5 magnitudes, or 100 times brighter at opposition than near conjunction! In its swiftest part, the change can occur at better than three-quarters a magnitude a month, which is fast enough for a difference in the brightness of Mars to be noticed literally every week. At perihelic oppositions, Mars is likely to outshine Jupiter for a while

123

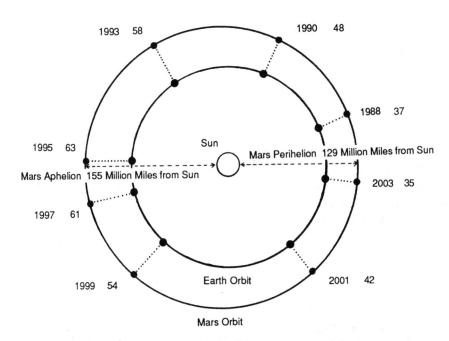

Figure 20 Orbits of Mars and Earth, Showing Mars's Oppositions.
Numbers next to years are Earth–Mars distances in millions of miles.

and be surpassed in brightness only by Venus, which we can never see high in the midnight heavens.

The 15 or 17 years between perihelic oppositions of Mars is even greater than the time between edgewise presentations of Saturn's rings. Between two perihelic oppositions, there is at first a steady progress through more distant oppositions until aphelic opposition, at which time the progress goes the other way.

The increase in the size of Mars during a perihelic apparition is easily the greatest of any of the planets. The disk can become about 25 arc-seconds across (bigger than Saturn ever appears but smaller than Jupiter). This is about 8 times wider than when Mars is smallest. It is also almost 2 times as wide as at an aphelic opposition. But this last statement does not really tell the whole story. There seems to be a kind of critical distance for viewing Mars: Beyond the distance, only a few features are likely to be glimpsed in amateur telescopes; within the distance, dozens are revealed in the best moments of "seeing." Many oppositions do not bring Mars to the critical distance, or, if so, merely to the verge of it briefly.

Unfortunately, all but the very start and the end of the 1990s is a period where Mars does not get very close to Earth. Table 7 is based on data in

Table 7
Mars's Oppositions, 1988–2005*

Opposition	Magnitude	Altitudes§	Nearest Earth	Distance**	Size§§
1988 Sep 27	−2.7	48°	1988 Sep 21	37	24
1990 Nov 27	−2.0	73°	1990 Nov 19	48	18
1993 Jan 7	−1.4	76°	1993 Jan 3	58	15
1995 Feb 11	−1.2	68°	1995 Feb 11	63	14
1997 Mar 17	−1.3	55°	1997 Mar 20	61	14
1999 Apr 24	−1.7	38°	1999 May 1	54	16
2001 Jun 13	−2.3	23°	2001 Jun 21	42	21
2003 Aug 28	−2.9	34°	2003 Aug 27	35	25
2005 Nov 7	−2.3	66°	2005 Oct 29	43	20

* Data derived from Abrams Planetarium's *Sky Calendar*.

§ Angular altitude at highest (middle of night) as seen from 40°N latitude.

** Distance of Mars from Earth in millions of miles.

§§ Maximum disk diameter of Mars in arc-seconds.

the Abrams Planetarium's *Sky Calendar* (see the "Sources of Information" section for details on this excellent publication). It shows that not until 2001 will the brightness and disk size that Mars had in 1990 be surpassed—and for viewers at mid-northern latitudes of Earth, the Red Planet will appear very low in the sky at that 2001 event. The truly perihelic opposition of 2003 will bring Mars a little closer to Earth than it has come in thousands of years.

We must make the most we can out of the poorer oppositions of Mars. Each opposition presents its own special sights, thanks to the variety of the angles at which the planet is tilted toward us and the, in some cases, unpredictable details of the seasonal phenomena (see Table 8 in Activity 41 for a calendar of the Martian seasons in the 1990s). But, at each opposition of Mars, the observer can keep track of just how well various features were able to be seen and can compare oppositions. It ought to be possible to say that a particular feature, if not significantly changed by dust-storm activity, should be visible in roughly a certain size of telescope when Mars reaches a certain diameter.

In addition, there are particular especially difficult observations that you can plan to try at the very best Martian oppositions—or if you ever have access to a very large telescope. One is the search for the largest topographic features, as opposed to just *albedo* (dark and light) features, on Mars (see Activity 40).

Another is the hunt for the eerie little moons of Mars. Phobos (see Figure 21) and Deimos are irregularly shaped moons whose average diameters are, respectively, 13 miles (21 km) and 7 miles (12 km). Their magnitudes at very good oppositions are about 11 for Phobos and 12 for Deimos. But these strange worldlets orbit so near to Mars that seeing them is difficult in the planet's glare, although it is possible to see them with as small as a 6- or 8-inch telescope at an excellent opposition. Since Phobos is never farther than about one Mars-diameter from the edge of Mars, dimmer Deimos is easier to spot. Very clean optics, knowledge of where the moons are, and some kind of strip of opaque material in your eyepiece to hide Mars are almost essential. Will even large amateur telescopes show these moons at the poorer oppositions of the 1990s? The article on observing Phobos and Deimos in the December 1990 issue of *Sky & Telescope* gives you a hint: "Our next guide to finding the moons of Mars isn't scheduled until the issue of June, 2001!"

Questions

1. What are the sights visible in the current apparition of Mars that might not be visible in any other for a long time? What are the special aspects of the planet's tilt toward us and of the planet's seasonal activity?

2. How do the features visible at the next opposition of Mars compare with what is or might be visible at the farther ones of the mid-1990s and the closer ones thereafter until 2003? For each combination of Mars's apparent diameter and telescope size, what are the surface features that begin to become visible?

39.

The Dark Surface Features of Mars

Identify as many of the dark surface features of Mars as possible each night. Do a series of sketches over a period of several hours to demonstrate the rotation of Mars and see how foreshortening of features far from the central meridian affects their appearance.

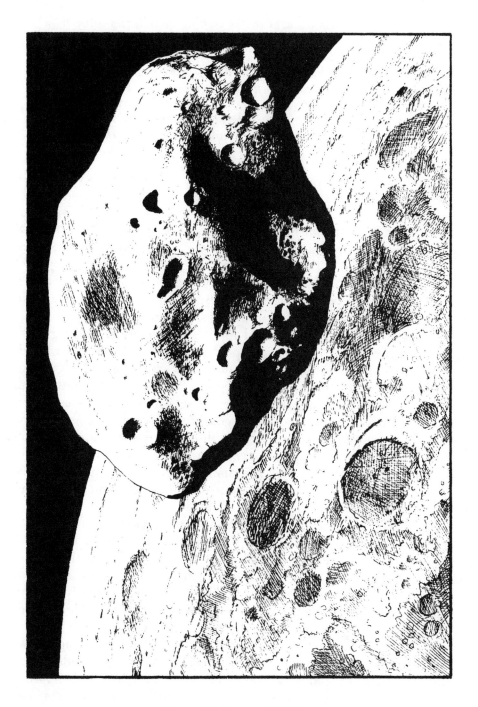

Figure 21 Mars and Phobos.

Try to ascertain what changes in the shifting boundaries between light and dark features have occurred since the map shown in Figure 22 was made in 1986. Watch for the "wave of darkening" and rate how much higher the contrast of features gets during the course of its progression. Look for other changes in the features during months or even weeks of the current apparition, distinguishing between temporary dust-storm cloud obscurations and longer-term changes in the actual boundaries of the dark areas.

Only on Mars do we get surface features that are sometimes easy to observe. Only on Mars are we (even amateur astronomers with modest telescopes) able to see both surface features and clouds (in fact, a variety of both) and thereby learn far more than we can about any other planet. Of course, for reasons discussed in the previous activity, seeing even a few features of Mars (let alone the dozens that are perceptible when the planet comes unusually near) is often not possible. And, even at the best of times, observing Mars well is a real challenge. But if there is any challenge in planetary observation worth great effort, surely this is it.

In observing Mars, most of what appears on the disk are dark (grayish tending to greenish in larger telescopes) areas and light (ocher-colored) areas of the actual surface. The dark markings are essentially regions of rock and coarser dirt; the light areas, regions of fine dust. The latter is so plentiful and so ably transported on the thin yet often swift Martian winds that the areas of dark and light change considerably over the course of the long Martian seasons and years. Even with this provision added, the fact remains that most of the major surface features of Mars can be easily identified again and again. Moreover, the changes are simple enough to follow and study—in fact, to be potentially quite enlightening about the Martian surface and climate.

The map of the Martian dark and light markings in Figure 22 shows what they looked like in 1986. It is obvious that at one time only half of the features on the map are on the hemisphere of Mars facing Earth, but it is well to remember that far less than half of the features are placed near enough to the central meridian of Mars so as to be seen clearly without foreshortening. You can look up the longitude of the central meridian of Mars for different dates and times each year in the *Astronomical Almanac* or, when Mars is near opposition, in the popular astronomy magazines.

Even without consulting these publications, you may (under good conditions) be able to identify a prominent feature and then study how fast it moves across the face of the Red Planet. You will find that the rotation period of Mars is about 24 hours, 37½ minutes. This means that any feature that you observe on the central meridian of Mars tonight will be

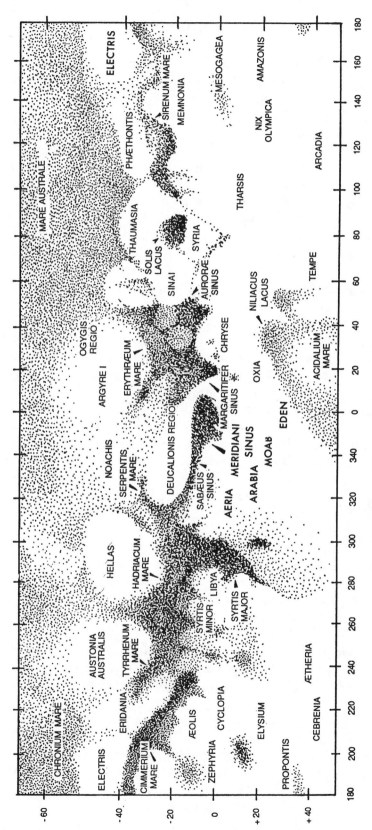

Figure 22 Map of Martian Surface Features in 1986.

there again about 37½ minutes later on each succeeding night. This is convenient for observing a feature at roughly the same part of the night for several nights in a row, but afterward you will find that you must wait 36 days to get the feature back on the central meridian at the original time. If Mars is above the horizon in only the evening or only the morning hours, the feature may not be possible for you to see at any time of night, convenient or otherwise, for weeks. Fortunately for Mars research, other longitudes of Earth will in such cases have the feature of interest pointed toward them at the correct time so that it can be observed.

You will notice that the map in Figure 22 shows the range from only a little south of $-60°$ to a little north of $+40°$ latitude on Mars. For several reasons, this is not much of a defect. One reason is, of course, that the poles of Mars are never inclined anything like face-on to Earth—we always get a considerably foreshortened view, and the higher the latitude the more the foreshortening. A more interesting reason for the coverage being farther in the south is that the far-northern latitudes of Mars are never seen as well as the southern. This results from the fact that near Mars's perihelion point, the southern hemisphere of the Red Planet is always the one tilted toward the Sun and thus toward the Earth if Mars is at a perihelic (or nearly perihelic) opposition. (This peculiarity of the Martian seasons leads to some dramatic differences between the north and south polar ice caps of Mars. These caps are the topic of Activity 41.)

If a polar cap is well placed enough and large enough, it can easily be the most prominent feature on Mars. But the most prominent dark marking is often that which Christiaan Huygens was able to identify even with the poor optics of the mid-seventeenth century—triangular Syrtis Major. Other features like Cimmerium Mare, Tyrrhenum Mare, Sirenum Mare, Sabaeus Sinus, Meridiani Sinus, and Solis Lacus become familiar sights to observers of Mars as the planet rotates each around to become the dominant marking on that particular face. But a few of these features, it should be remembered, are often altered dramatically by dust-storm activity. This is spectacularly true of Solis Lacus (Lake of the Sun), which only at some apparitions has the prominence and form to deserve its title as "the Eye of Mars."

Quite apart from temporary obscurations by dust storms, there are longer-lasting changes in the boundaries between the dark regions and the light ones. Study your sketches carefully to see what changes you think you can ascertain.

There are many changes in the features of Mars and in many of the dark markings that are extremely subtle. Consequently, particular care is needed in the sketching of Mars. Pointers about drawing Mars are given in the next activity, as are tips about filters, another assistance to observers.

But I would like to conclude this first part of our survey of the surface features of Mars with comment on the most sensational of all the systematic changes that happen to the dark features.

I refer to a marvelous phenomenon by which the dark features of Mars grow darker in appearance. It occurs in the spring and summer hemisphere as the ice cap melts. This *wave of darkening* was not understood until comparatively recently. For decades, there was suspicion that it was caused by the growth of new vegetation on Mars each spring! Finally, there was vindication for Charles Capen's claim that the wave of darkening was really a "wave of brightening" of the ocher-colored areas that made the dark features look darker by improved contrast. We now know that the melting of frost in spring reveals fresh, brighter deposits of the ocher dust moved by the previous year's dust storms. You can estimate the strength of the wave of darkening as it proceeds from pole toward equator by using a 1-to-10 scale, with 1 as the lowest contrast between dark and light areas and 10 as the highest.

A phenomenon profoundly different from the wave of darkening, although it too makes features more prominent (but only at certain wavelengths), is the violet clearing, which is discussed in Activity 42.

Questions

1. How many of the dark features on the map in Figure 22 can you identify on Mars? How different do they look when they are far from the central meridian and foreshortened? Can you produce a series of sketches showing the different faces of Mars around the full range of Martian longitudes? A series of sketches showing the progress of a feature across the face of Mars?

2. Can you document the different stages of the wave of darkening? How much contrast with their bright surroundings, rated on a 1-to-10 scale, do various features get at each of the stages?

3. What changes in the dark markings since the map in Figure 22 was made in 1986 can you demonstrate? What changes during the months of the current apparition?

4. How large a telescope and what atmospheric conditions on Earth do you need before you start glimpsing a greenish hue in the dark regions? Is there any way to determine to what extent the green is created by contrast with the ocher-colored light areas of Mars?

40.

The Light and the Topographic Surface Features of Mars

Try to find through the telescope as many of the light regions on the Mars map in Figure 22 as possible. Locate and observe Hellas, Argyre I, and Chryse. Watch for frost or dust clouds in Hellas. If you have a good opposition of Mars and / or a large telescope, try to locate the greatest topographic features, including Olympus Mons and the other Tharsis volcanoes as well as some part of the Valles Marineris. Practice trying to sketch Mars accurately in the standard way. Note what effects your use of orange and red filters has on the visibility of Martian surface features.

We continue here with the second part of our examination of the Martian surface features. The dusty, light-colored plains and basins of Mars are not so easy to differentiate from one another, for they are sometimes separated by very subtle dark borderings (and perhaps sometimes not even that!).

You may want to try at least looking in the general area of the plain of Chryse (the plain of "gold"), where in 1976 the Viking 1 Lander made the first soft-touchdown on the planet Mars. That spacecraft was the first to show us from the surface the pink skies and blue sunsets, and the red rocks of this magnificent wilderness world.

You should also look for the two great southerly impact basins, Hellas and Argyre (Argyre I). The former is an awesome feature about 1,000 miles (1,600 km) across. Its "rim" is very eroded, but its depth of 3 miles (5 km) is enough to make Hellas the lowest point on the planet Mars and also to render it especially visible from Earth in southern winter by virtue of the bright coating of frost that can gather in its vast bowl. Since Hellas is also a great birthplace of major dust storms, it can turn golden, too. Argyre is better preserved than Hellas but is much smaller at 360 miles (600 km) across.

Hellas and Argyre are seen by virtue of their difference in lightness from the darker regions around them, not by virtue of shadows in them or any other cue that would be a direct indication of their being relief features (unless you consider Hellas's frosts a "direct" indication). A few other famous topographic features of Mars can be glimpsed in a similar way.

One example is mighty Olympus Mons. It was once known as Nix

Olympica ("Snows of Olympus") because it was sighted as a bright area. Astronomers were probably seeing clouds surrounding its exposed (thus darker-looking) summit. I have one friend, a skilled observer, who has apparently seen the darkness outlining the mountain mass itself (the periphery of the mountain has a fairly steep drop-off, even though from there the rise to the summit is extremely shallow). His instrument was an excellent 6-inch Newtonian telescope! But this was at the perihelic opposition of 1988, as were his and a few other observers' claimed sightings of part of the enormous Valles Marineris. Could these features (and the other great Tharsis volcanoes) be glimpsed with larger telescopes at poorer oppositions? My friend has expressed the opinion that perhaps all the albedo features of Mars that can be glimpsed can be glimpsed with as little as a 6-inch telescope under excellent "seeing" when the planet is at a very good opposition (not all the detail within them, though—as proven by the sensational CCD images of Mars obtained in 1988). But surely only a few topographic features can be seen from Earth.

These ultimate challenges of seeing Martian topographic features remind one of the "canals" of Mars that Percival Lowell made so famous. Ironically, none of these canals was the Valles Marineris. But in recent years, photographs taken from Earth have shown that the dark lines which Lowell perceived were not all subjective. Notice, for instance, the ones sometimes seen around Solis Lacus. These seemingly continuous linear features are, however, shown by sharper imagery and observations under the very best "seeing" to be composed of smaller, separate splotches of dark terrain.

Two things can assist greatly your observations of all the surface features of Mars: (1) proper sketching and (2) filters.

As I have stressed several times in this book, sketching is not just a tool for giving you a permanent and shareable record of your observations, it is the best way to improve your observing abilities. And with no celestial object is this more true, and your improvement more valuable, than with the planet Mars.

The standard sizes of blank Mars disks (which, of course, you should prepare in advance) are 2 inches or 42 mm. These are the only sizes, for instance, that ALPO can examine with their coordinate-grid overlays. Other important things to remember are to first draw in the phase effect (if any is observable) on Mars, and to note the time of the sketch carefully. Although the rotation period of Mars is almost $2\frac{1}{2}$ times longer than that of Jupiter or Saturn, you will have to be careful about how long you take. If you need quite a while (trying to wait to get more and more of those magical glimpses in moments of good "seeing"), you should write down the time you began and ended.

Nothing can surpass the benefits of having a trained eye, but filters are a tremendous help in viewing Mars. Red and orange filters are the ones to try. In our next two activities, we will see that other kinds of filters are useful for viewing the polar caps and various Martian atmospheric phenomena more clearly. But if you want to perceive the dark markings of Mars with greater contrast, then red and orange filters are the choice. Mars is very bright when it is well placed (its albedo or reflectivity is less than that of the clouds of Jupiter or Saturn, but the sunlight shining on it is stronger). But make sure your filter does not dim the planet so much as to defeat its purpose and reduce the visibility of subtle features.

Questions

1. How many of the light regions on the map in Figure 22 can you identify? Do any of the light features you sketch turn out to be Martian clouds?
2. Can you find Hellas, Argyre I, and Chryse? When do you note frost or dust clouds in Hellas?
3. Can you glimpse Olympus Mons or any part of the Valles Marineris directly, even with a large telescope at a good opposition?
4. How much improvement in visibility of various Martian features can you get by using various red and orange filters?

41.

The Polar Ice Caps of Mars

Follow the progress of each polar ice cap's melting (or restoration) and sketch each carefully. Determine, if Mars is visible and properly tilted at the time, when the smallest cap occurs. Look for the Mountains of Mitchel (Novus Mons) detachment of polar ice, as well as other rifts and subsequent detached areas, as the south cap melts. Determine how much green filters improve the visibility of features in the polar caps.

Sometimes, the most prominent feature on Mars is one of the planet's polar ice caps. A good view of one of these chillingly white patches would be memorable even if we were not aware of what this feature was (yet another striking similarity between our planet and Mars) and where it was (marking a pole of a world whose axial inclination and rotation period are remarkably like our own). But there is far more of interest and strangeness to know about these caps and the dramatic changes they go through before the eyes of any telescopic viewer who observes them during the course of an apparition.

The Martian polar caps are different from Earth's polar caps in several ways. First of all, they differ in composition. The Martian caps are composed not only of water ice but also of carbon dioxide ice. The latter is what we call "dry ice" because of its property of bypassing a liquid stage (going directly from solid to vapor) even at the fairly high atmospheric pressures on Earth (water ice does the same in Sun-warmed comets out in the vacuum of space). Since the temperature at which carbon dioxide unfreezes is much colder than that of water ice, it is the carbon dioxide component of the Martian caps that disappears first during Martian spring.

The atmosphere of Mars, which is only about $1/100$ as dense as Earth's atmosphere, is almost entirely carbon dioxide gas. About 20 percent of this atmosphere condenses to form the carbon dioxide component of whichever pole is experiencing winter! While the air over the polar regions of Earth is very dry and most of the moisture in it tends to freeze and condense or fall to the surface, at least a sizable fraction of our entire atmosphere's major component, nitrogen, does not freeze and end up on the ground each winter!

The ice caps of Mars are certainly much thinner than Earth's caps (although exactly how thin is not known), and their extent varies far more greatly. But the question of how greatly brings us to the matter of how much the north and south caps of Mars themselves differ.

The greater warmth of Mars's southern-hemisphere summer (due to the fact that it occurs when Mars is around perihelion) and the greater cold of its southern-hemisphere winter (due to the fact that it occurs around aphelion) lead to some important differences between the north and south polar ice caps. The north cap never melts entirely; its water ice part remains while the carbon dioxide ice part evaporates. But the more extreme winter and summer seasons at the south pole mean that its extent can vary far more greatly than that of the north pole. In winter, the south cap can stretch to about $-60°$ latitude as opposed to the north's maximum spread to about $+65°$. (These are only averages, and isolated patches of very thin carbon dioxide frost can be found much farther north or south as proven by the Voyager 2 images at 48° north.) In many summers, the south polar ice cap dwindles to a diminutive patch, offset about 4° from the geographic pole and smaller than the north cap ever gets. And in some summers—as a telescopic observer can see for himself or herself—the south cap melts away entirely.

In looking at the ice caps of Mars, you cannot help thinking about the question of water on Mars and the related question of life. The Mariner 9 spacecraft and the Viking Orbiters photographed numerous and sometimes huge features that can only be dry riverbeds. The patterns of dried mud around some impact craters are among the evidence that rather large quantities of water are stored not far below the Martian surface in the form of permafrost. In the past few years, new theories suggest that not only great rivers and great floods but also considerable Martian oceans may have once existed (the planet is now all land—as much as the entire land area of Earth, since about three-quarters of our larger planet is water-covered). Although pessimism about the possibility of native Martian life remains (the Viking Lander soil tests were negative, and the ultraviolet radiation that bathes the surface breaks down the building blocks of incipient life), the book is by no means yet closed.

In winter, a strong haze spreads over the northern polar cap. Observers should study it and its timing in relation to the cap's development and the season, in the hope of finding some clues about it. The perihelic summer and aphelic winter of the south cap, and reverse of the north cap, are probably responsible for all the differences between the caps, but just how they are responsible is not understood in all the cases. Why is there, for instance, the vastest field of dunes in the solar system (covering an area very much larger than Earth's Sahara Desert) in the north polar region but not the south polar region of Mars? We do know that the north polar cap is dustier and less reflective, probably because it condenses from the atmosphere during the time when the greatest amounts of dust are in the air from south-hemisphere summer-caused heating.

Stranger than the great dunefields between 70° and 80°N are the areas of "layered terrain" above 80° latitude at both poles. These are, as Ron Miller and William K. Hartmann have put it, "like a giant's staircase." These steps range from about 30 feet to 160 feet (10 m to 50 m) high, with some individual steps extending laterally for hundreds of miles. They must have been built up from deposits of dust and ice (at the north pole they are now always covered with ice), sculpted by the mighty winds spiraling around the poles. The patterns of these deposits and winds have changed in regular fashion over thousands or millions of years with the cyclic changes in Mars's orbit and axial inclination. We may have here the blueprint of Mars's past laid out before us—if only we can learn to read it!

Although the dunes and the layered terrain are beyond the direct reach of earthbound eyes, the melting away of the caps in spring and summer is full of intricacies, and is never quite the same. With excellent "seeing" and high magnification, delicate rifts in the melting caps can be seen, and these broaden to give rise to detached sections of ice. The most famous detachment starts out as a projection of the ice cap and is then called Novissima Thyle, but when it becomes entirely separated is known as the "Mountains of Mitchel," or Novus Mons. Rather than being an elevated region, it is thought to be a depressed area in which the ice lingers. Novus Mons and other features of the melting south polar ice cap are shown in Figure 23.

Of course, a good view of a particular polar cap will only be obtained if the cap is tilted relatively well toward Earth when the planet is not too many months from opposition. Table 8 lists what is best tilted at each opposition of Mars in the 1990s and shows how the dates of these oppositions fall in relation to the times of perihelion and the times of Martian north- and south-hemisphere midsummers.

Whereas orange and red filters are best for improving the visibility of the dark markings of Mars, green filters can help with observations of details in the polar caps.

Questions

1. What is revealed by your sketches showing the development of a Martian polar ice cap's melt? When is the progress most rapid? How much of the cap is left when it reaches its minimum, and what time in what Martian season does this occur?

2. When does the polar hood of haze begin to appear over the north polar cap? When does it disappear? When the south cap melts, do you detect the Mountains of Mitchel? How does this detachment proceed—that is, what do your sketches show? What other rifts and detached areas do you observe?

3. What improvement in visibility of polar features do you (or do you not) obtain with the use of green filters?

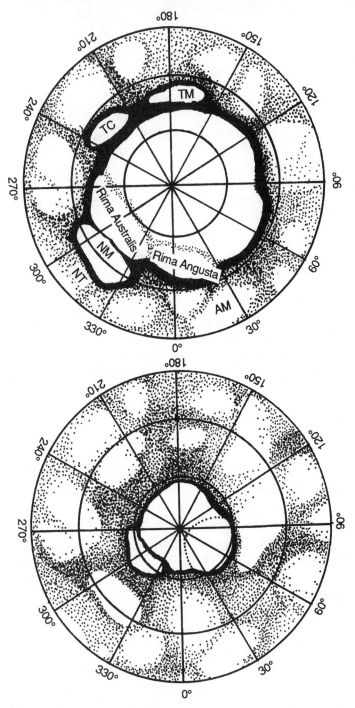

Figure 23 Maps of Mars's South Polar Ice Cap in 1986. (Adapted by Doug Myers from the original maps of Jeff Beish.) The figures around the edge are Martian longitude; the circles are Martian latitude at 10° intervals. The upper map shows the region in Martian midspring. The lower map shows the region in Martian early summer, and the dotted area is the off-center remnant of the cap left in late summer. Abbreviations: NM—Novus Mons; NT—Novissima Thyle; TM—Thyles Mons; TC—Thyles Collis; AM—Argenteus Mons.

Table 8
Martian Perihelion, Solstice, and Equinox Dates and Presentation
of Disk at Opposition, 1990–2000

Year	Opposition	Favored*	Peri.§	Spr. Equinox**	Sum. Solstice**
1990	Nov 27	S. Pole (sl.)	Jul 1	Mar 6 (S)	Jul 30 (S)
1991				Jan 4	Jul 22
1992			May 18	Nov 21	
1993	Jan 7	Equator			Jun 8
1994			Apr 4	Oct 9	
1995	Feb 11	N. Pole			Apr 26
1996			Feb 21	Aug 26	
1997	Mar 17	N. Pole (max.)			Mar 13
1998			Jan 8	Jul 14	
1999	Apr 24	N. Pole			Jan 29
2000			Nov 25	May 31	Dec 16

* Part of Mars tilted favorably toward Earth. Abbreviation "sl." means pole is slightly tilted toward Earth; "max." means pole is at maximum tilt toward Earth.

§ Date of perihelion.

** Dates of spring equinox and summer solstice in northern hemisphere of Mars, except where noted "S" for southern-hemisphere spring equinox and summer solstice.

42.

Atmospheric Phenomena of Mars

Look for orographic clouds (W-clouds), noting the time of Martian day and season of their occurrence and the improvement of their visibility with a violet or blue filter. Watch for and observe limb hazes and limb clouds, trying to determine their altitude by the use of different filters. Use different filters to try to identify which "bright patches" are fogs and which are frosts. Note where and when fogs and frosts appear and disappear. Search, with or without filters, for yellow dust clouds, and note their location and time of season. Track the development and movement of dust clouds carefully. Using a violet filter, keep vigil for a violet clearing. When one is observed, note how it develops, when and where it occurs, and any other circumstances that might help explain it.

As tenuous as the atmosphere of Mars is, it is a lively medium and is connected with the land and ice of the planet intricately and profoundly. Much of the weather of Mars is set in motion by the melting and recondensation of the polar caps. The greater dust storms, stirred by the winds from the heating of southern-hemisphere summer, have tremendous effects from pole to pole—poles that they help to make so different from each other.

Amateur study of the Martian atmosphere has almost everything in its favor. It requires only a fairly small telescope (and, preferably, a few filters). It offers great variety, with a number of different kinds of clouds and other atmospheric phenomena in many different situations. It offers great mystery, with many of the questions most likely to be answered by exactly what amateur astronomers can best provide—the many man-hours and woman-hours of vigilant watching by a large network of enthusiastic observers. Last but not least, study of Martian atmospheric phenomena is of great practical importance to humanity's plans to pick the best site and ensure personal safety when citizens of the planet Earth visit, and then colonize, the planet Mars.

The weather of Mars has in recent years been a major topic of study for ALPO. An excellent article on observing Mars, with comprehensive coverage of the "Martian weather project" and a "weather map of Mars," appeared in the April 1988 issue of *Sky & Telescope*. The authors were Jeff Beish and Donald Parker, who are, with Carlos E. Hernandez, the ALPO Mars Recorders. Beish's map is based on over 12,000 observations from 1963 to 1987 and shows the preferred areas of Martian clouds, fogs and frosts, and dust clouds. What follows here are notes about some of the principal Martian weather phenomena that amateur astronomers can hope to study.

Orographic Clouds (also called W-Clouds). Orographic clouds are a well-known type on Earth. They occur when moist air encounters a mountain and is lifted and cooled so that the moisture condenses to form visible clouds. When they occur on Mars, these clouds are always seen in the lee of the Martian volcanoes, the mightiest of which are Olympus Mons and the three other great Tharsis volcanoes, Ascraeus Mons, Pavonis Mons, and Arsia Mons. The combination of several such clouds near these neighboring mountains gave rise to the W-shape that led to these clouds' earlier name. The orographic clouds form in spring and summer in the moister air caused by a polar cap's melting. They also form in the afternoon, which on Mars is toward the leading side (the celestial west) of the planet's disk as it floats across the field of view of a telescope that has its clock drive turned off. The orographic clouds are better seen with the use of blue and violet filters.

Limb Hazes and Limb Clouds. These are seen along the sunrise and sunset edges of the planet, appearing as bright, sometimes bluish arcs (the clouds are smaller and brighter than the hazes). What we are seeing is clouds and haze composed of carbon dioxide ice crystals, water ice crystals, dust, or a combination of these. Why we see it rather well is that we are looking through a longer pathway of atmosphere here and thus a greater total amount of material. Various filters may be useful—violet for the highest haze and clouds, blue-green or orange for the lower.

Fogs and Frosts. These are often considered together as "bright patches," for indeed it may be difficult to tell at just how low an altitude the patch is (the best diagnosis is with the filters used for limb hazes and limb clouds). Fogs usually occur in valleys and basins (also on up-slopes); frosts, in many places, including both basins and mountains. Both fogs and frosts, especially the former, are most likely to be seen in the early morning part of Mars.

Yellow Dust Clouds. These yellow spots may appear in various places, but the most common, and most likely to be the start of a major dust storm, are northwest of Hellas in the Serpentis–Noachis region, around Solis Lacus, and in Chryse. Great planetwide dust storms, which hide all surface features on Mars, have been documented only at the near-perihelion oppositions of 1956, 1971, and 1973 (all observed from Earth, with the 1971 storm initially hiding Mars from the newly arrived Mariner 9), as well as twice in 1977 (discovered by the Viking orbiters). No dust storms of this magnitude were seen in 1986 or 1988, and it may be that they are less common than was thought a few years ago. Minor dust storms are common, however, and Jeff Beish has demonstrated that dust storms have not one but three different peak times of occurrence—the southern-hemisphere seasons of late spring (after perihelion), midsummer, and early winter. Whenever you see a yellow patch—or perhaps just notice that a part of a dark marking disappeared since the previous day or week you observed—you should take the utmost care to study and sketch its development and movement. The filters to use for making early detection of the clouds, and then to see them well, are yellow, orange, and red.

The Viking missions and the work of numerous amateur astronomers have in recent years solved a number of the mysteries of the Martian atmosphere. But a large number of questions remain. And there is one mystery that seems to have resisted all attempts to explain it—the *violet clearing*.

Normally, a look at Mars through a violet filter is capable of showing little more than the highest clouds. But sometimes, for maybe just a few days, the view changes, revealing the dark markings of Mars plainly through the filter. Your observations might be as likely as anyone's to help provide some clue to this mysterious phenomenon.

Questions

1. Can you spot orographic or W-clouds? Which part of which Martian season do you see them? Which part of the Martian day? How much does a violet filter improve their visibility?

2. What are the details of the structure of any limb hazes or limb clouds you see? Do they seem to be associated with any dust storm activity? Using various filters as described in this activity, can you determine whether the haze or cloud is high, medium-high, or low? Can you make the same use of filters to distinguish whether any "bright patches" you see on the disk of Mars are clouds, fogs, or frosts? Where do you find these phenomena, and at what season and time of day?

3. With or without filters, can you find any dust clouds? Where have they originated from? Where are they spreading to? How do their size and shape change over the course of the days you watch them? What time of the Martian season are they occurring? What time in relation to the planet's reaching perihelion?

4. Can you witness a violet clearing? How localized is it? If it starts out localized, where and how does it spread? What is the time of Martian season? What have the polar caps been doing recently and how might this be related to the clearing? What clouds, fogs, or frosts have you observed around the time of the violet clearing?

43.

Apparitions of Mercury

Try to estimate what the color of Mercury's disk is on various occasions, noting its altitude and your observing conditions. Attempt to find it as near to the times of superior and inferior conjunction as possible and also for as many days and as many apparitions as possible each year. Observe Mercury near greatest elongation and see whether you note any lapse between this time and the time it is at dichotomy.

Mercury is the most neglected of the planets. Sometimes brighter than the brightest star, possessed of the only planetary surface other than the Martian surface that we can see, Mercury is regarded by most amateur astronomers as being too close to the Sun to be an appropriate object for an observing program.

But the difficulty of finding it, as well as the difficulty of getting a steady image of its disk down low where "seeing" is always worse, has been exaggerated. Mercury is a challenge, to be sure, but there is a big difference between a challenge and a hopeless case.

Mercury used to be thought of as the smallest planet, the hottest planet—and also the coldest planet, due to the (mistaken) belief that it always kept one face pointed away from the Sun. We now know that Pluto is the coldest and the smallest, and Venus, with its extreme greenhouse effect, is the hottest. A distinction that Mercury will never lose, however, is that of the innermost and the fastest planet.

These characteristics are what make it so elusive for observers. It is an "inferior planet" (closer in to the Sun than Earth is), like Venus, and goes through the same order of major events: superior conjunction on the far side of the Sun, greatest eastern elongation in the evening sky, inferior conjunction on the near side of the Sun, greatest western elongation in the morning sky, and then back to superior conjunction. But, whereas Venus can pull out to 47° from the Sun and set 4 hours after (or rise 4 hours before) the Sun at its best apparitions, Mercury can manage only 28° (at best), and for only a few days a year may set a few minutes after the end of evening twilight (or rise a few minutes before the start of morning twilight). Mercury can never really be seen properly in a fully dark sky.

Actually, the surface brightness of Mercury is great enough that we do not want to see it through the telescope against a fully dark sky. The real problem is that if you wait until after sunset to find Mercury in the twilight sky, the planet is so low that "seeing" is usually bad.

One possible solution is to observe Mercury after sunset (or before sunrise) often enough to catch the few occasions when "seeing" is reasonably good even down low in the sky. The other solution is to observe Mercury high in broad daylight—but this will take some real work. You can review our discussion of observing Venus in the daytime. But you should know that Mercury will be a more difficult target to find in the daytime. Mercury has a much lower surface brightness than Venus (although sunlight on Mercury is stronger, the reflectivity of Mercury's dark rocks is many times less than that of Venus's light clouds). And, Mercury will usually appear closer to the Sun and thus in a brighter area of sky—you will have to observe on very clear, haze-free days, when the Sun has no more than a small *aureole* of scattered light around it. The greater proximity to the Sun also means that you will have to be even more careful about not getting the blinding solar disk in your field of view, especially if you try scanning. Actually, you are quite unlikely to find Mercury by simply knowing its elongation from the Sun and scanning (although I have seen this feat performed). The method of using setting circles is almost imperative.

Mercury and Venus are very different planets. Even their color shows it. Whereas the clouds of Venus are very distinctly yellow, the color of Mercury ought to be whitish or really a neutral gray. Often, however, Mercury seems to have an orange tinge. Could this be any more than the effect of haze at the low altitude at which it is usually observed? Check the color of Mercury on many occasions, especially when it is in close conjunction with another planet.

One similarity of the apparitions of Mercury and Venus is that not all are equally good for observers at a given latitude. But the difference between good and bad Mercury apparitions, however, is far greater and more critical.

The first reason is orbital eccentricity. In our era, Venus has the most nearly circular of all planetary orbits. Mercury has the least circular after that of Pluto. Greatest elongations of Venus vary between 45° and 47°; greatest elongations of Mercury vary between 17° and 28°. Strangely enough, however, the elongation in itself is not crucial. For an observer at mid-northern latitudes on Earth, the minimum greatest elongation of Mercury could be the year's best. What matters is the time of year because it determines the angle of the ecliptic (roughly the angle of the planet's rising or setting) with respect to the horizon. At mid-northern latitudes, the angle of the ecliptic is steep around spring equinox in the dusk sky and around autumn equinox in the dawn sky. So the best evening apparitions of Mercury (also of Venus) thus tend to be those near spring equinox; the best morning apparitions, those near autumn equinox. At such times, a planet's elongation can be almost vertical at sunset; its angular altitude, virtually as large as its elongation.

How poor is a poor apparition of Mercury? Poor enough for the planet not to be seen at all with the naked eye. A good apparition features Mercury easily visible and setting over 1½ hours after the Sun (or rising this long before the Sun) around the time of greatest elongation. The statement usually made is that Mercury can be seen about two weeks before and one week after a greatest evening elongation at a good apparition—so quick is this planet in its true movements around the Sun! But how many observers try viewing Mercury during this entire period, or for even longer? Most don't—and should.

Mercury really can be seen for more nights and more apparitions than the average amateur astronomer thinks. Trying to see Mercury at a fairly poor apparition, besides being a chance to test and opportunity to sharpen your skills, might actually pay off in showing you features of a face of Mercury very rarely seen. Trying to see more of a Mercury apparition could have the same result, and certainly will provide you with a look at Mercury's phases that few people have observed.

As an inferior planet, Mercury does of course show phases to observers on Earth. Our ability to see these phases and other aspects of observing them are strikingly different than they are with Venus.

Actually, the first sight of these planets after superior conjunction can be similar as to phase and even as to size. Although Venus is much bigger in real diameter, it is also at such times much farther from Earth. But you will find observing Mercury when it is still almost fully lit far more difficult than doing so with Venus because Mercury then is still at such a small elongation. A remarkable difference is that at this stage, not long after superior conjunction in the evening (or not long before superior conjunction in the morning), Mercury appears brightest. Venus, you may recall, is brightest when it is about midway between greatest elongation and inferior conjunction. The reason for the difference? Simply that the distance between Earth and Venus can vary much more greatly than the distance between Earth and Mercury—Mercury's distance varies by about a factor of 2; that of Venus, by a factor of 6. Mercury's increase in apparent diameter as it approaches us cannot make up for its dwindling phase for long. And as Mercury's phase shrinks rapidly in the week or two before inferior conjunction, its magnitude dims spectacularly—sometimes to levels so low that it would appear as a dim object even in a midnight sky, let alone a bright twilight one.

Despite the smallness of Mercury (about 6 arc-seconds) when it is bright and the dimness of it when it is large (well, relatively large—up to

12 arc-seconds)—and the nearness of it to the Sun at both times!—these are phases of Mercury that still deserve to be studied and are not.

There are rare times when it is easier to see Mercury right at inferior conjunction than just before or after. How can this be? See Figure 24. I am referring to *transits* of Mercury, the passages of Mercury directly in front of the Sun as seen from Earth. Although rare, fortunately they are not as rare as transits of Venus. See Table 9 for details.

Table 9
Transits of Mercury and Venus

MERCURY, 1991–2019

Date	Time*	Duration§	Least Distance**
1993 Nov 6	3:58	1h, 40m	−928
1999 Nov 15§§	21:43	0h, 52m	+963
2003 May 7	7:53	5h, 18m	+709
2006 Nov 8	21:42	4h, 58m	−423
2016 May 9	15:00	7h, 30m	−319
2019 Nov 11	15:22	5h, 29m	+77

(No more transits of Mercury after 2019 until 2032)

VENUS, 1874–2125

Date	Time*	Duration§	Least Distance**
1874 Dec 9	4:02	4h, 40m	+825
1882 Dec 6	17:04	6h, 18m	−639
2004 Jun 8	8:24	6h, 12m	−628
2012 Jun 6	1:36	7h, 40m	+553
2117 Dec 11	2:51	5h, 41m	+721
2125 Dec 8	16:01	5h, 31m	−740

(No more transits of Venus after 2125 until 2247)

* Time of least angular distance between center of Sun's disk and center of planet's disk, in Ephemeris Time, which is within a few minutes of Universal Time (see "Note on the Measurement of Time, Position, Angular Distance, and Brightness in Astronomy"). If this time is during the day from your location, the transit will be visible, except in the case of the 1999 event (see note below).

§ Duration of transit from first (exterior) contact until last (exterior) contact, in hours and minutes.

** Least angular distance between Sun's center and planet's center, in arc-seconds.

§§ This 1999 event is a grazing transit, visible from only part of Earth.

Figure 24 Transits of Mercury and Venus. Note the ring of atmosphere around Venus.

Most observers have been lazy enough to settle for Mercury near greatest elongation, a time when its diameter is of average size and its phase is half lit. Or, is it half lit exactly on the day of greatest elongation? Careful observers have found a Schroter's effect with Mercury, too, but it is much less than that of Venus (see Activity 27). Although Mercury has no appreciable atmosphere at all, it is still not a perfectly smooth, uniformly surfaced ball. Find out whether you can detect a lapse in time between Mercury's greatest elongation and dichotomy.

Questions

1. What does Mercury's color appear to be on different nights? Can any orange or red tinge be attributed to haze down low in the sky?

2. Can you observe Mercury at every one of its six or seven apparitions in a year? How soon after and soon before superior conjunction can you observe it? Can you observe Mercury at its brightest? How soon after and soon before inferior conjunction can you observe it and to what thinness of crescent and to what largeness of diameter?

3. How soon before an evening greatest elongation or soon after a morning greatest elongation do you think Mercury is at dichotomy?

44.

Surface Features of Mercury

Look for surface features on Mercury, comparing your ability to glimpse them in daylight and twilight and in different sky conditions. Rate the likelihood that you are really seeing a feature you think you are, and try to observe it again over the next few days and weeks.

Something that hardly anyone remembers is that Mercury is often the closest planet to Earth. As little as it is in true diameter, its apparent diameter when it is most separated from the Sun is about 7 arc-seconds, which is larger than Mars usually appears. When "seeing" and other sky conditions are excellent, you can use 200X to 250X magnification on Mercury to make it look as large in your telescope as the Moon does to the naked eye.

Despite these considerations, the fact remains that the surface features of Mercury are difficult to glimpse. R. B. Minton has stated that the intrinsic contrast between Mercury's darker markings and the lighter background on the planet is about 20 percent but that scattered sunlight in our atmosphere during daytime observations makes the apparent contrast much less (about 8 percent and, for the weakest markings, maybe only 4 percent, this latter being about the eye's limit for distinguishing contrast under these conditions). So perhaps a twilight observation of Mercury during rare superb "seeing" might provide a better view of its surface features than one during daylight? This is a most interesting question to explore. When you do not have excellent "seeing," determine how much poorer your view of Mercury is by twilight than by daylight, relating it to some of your standard measures of "seeing."

Some authorities have given the impression that definite features cannot be glimpsed on Mercury by the amateur astronomer. They claim that the Mercury maps of professionals from Schiaparelli and Antoniadi up to the very eve of Mariner 10's 1974 and 1975 flybys do not correspond hardly at all with the features revealed by the spacecraft's photographs. But surely this is an exaggeration. Comparison of such photographs of topography to sketches (or the best Earth-based photos) of albedo features on Mercury is difficult. My own attempts at the comparison lead me to believe that there actually is some rather good agreement. Above all else, there is no doubt that real features can be glimpsed on Mercury—and, with the fine optics available to today's amateur astronomers, even fairly small telescopes can reveal them. There seems little doubt that some bright patches on Mercury seen by skilled observers really do correspond to the bright areas of rayed craters on the very Moonlike Mercurian surface. See Figure 25.

Of course, an observer must be cautious in judging what is seen on Mercury. As in observing Venus, it is quite possible to be deluded by optical effects, especially near Mercury's terminator. The blunting of the crescent horns of Mercury is now considered an optical effect. Antoniadi's belief that large areas of the planet could be obscured by whitish veils must also be rejected in light of what we now know about the tenuousness of the Mercurian atmosphere.

The best way to confirm the reality of features you think you see is to try following them over a number of nights. Do these features move with the rotation of the planet? This is very slow, although it does not require the 88 Earth-days once thought when astronomers believed that Mercury had synchronous rotation, the Mercurian day as long as the Mercurian year, Mercury always keeping the same face toward the Sun. Radar and then spacecraft studies have shown that the planet's rotation period is 58.65 days, which is two-thirds the length of the Mercurian year. Remarkably, this mathematical relationship works with several others to ensure that at the best apparitions of Mercury the planet always does present roughly the same hemisphere to Earth.

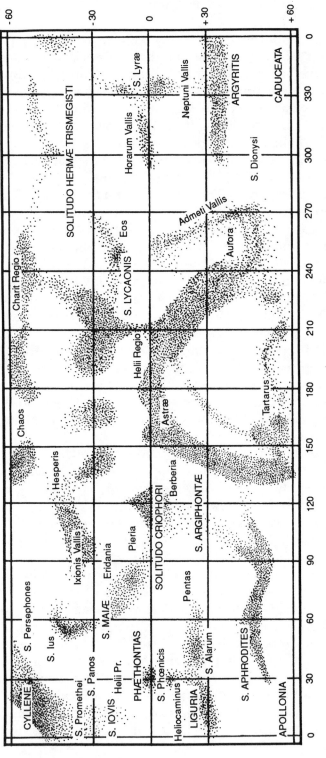

Figure 25 Map of Mercurian Surface Features. (Adapted by Doug Myers from the original by C. Chapman.)

Also surprising is the fact that the three flybys of Mariner 10 ended up permitting the spacecraft to photograph only one hemisphere of Mercury. It happened to be one that includes only part of the range of longitudes presented to Earth at the favorable apparitions. Thus, at least until around the turn of the century (when the USSR may send a spacecraft to Mercury), your views of parts of the planet may remain among the best that any human being has ever obtained!

Questions

1. How often do you suspect you are glimpsing surface features on Mercury? How much better can you detect them in daylight than in twilight? Can you discern them better in twilight than in daylight if "seeing" is superb?
2. How do your sketches compare with those of other observers (see Figure 25)?

45.

Uranus and Its Satellites

Determine how little light-gathering power suffices to show the color of Uranus and how little magnification suffices to show it as a disk. Find out the highest magnification you can ever use on Uranus and whether you even suspect you ever glimpse a detail on it. Compare the color of Uranus with that of Neptune and stars that it passes near. Observe close conjunctions of Uranus and stars, especially if close enough for an occultation of the star by a ring or moon (perhaps unknown) to be possible. Observe Titania and Oberon, tracking their motions over a number of nights.

Uranus is the most distant planet visible to the naked eye. It is about twice as far as Saturn, so when William Herschel discovered it in 1781 the diameter of the known solar system immediately doubled. There were prediscovery sightings of Uranus, but it was recorded as a star on maps for two reasons. First, the planet is so slow that no one was likely to notice its change of position even after a number of days. Second, the planet is so distant that even though it is 4 times the width of Earth it appears as a tiny disk, less than 4 arc-seconds across, in telescopes. With the poorer optics of his day, Herschel for some time presumed that the fuzzy-looking object whose motion he was following was a comet. Today, any amateur with a properly collimated 4- or 6-inch telescope on a night of decent "seeing" can tell that this little bluish green object is a definite dot, a tiny globe of a planet.

Most amateur astronomers are content just to confirm the identity of this object. But there are several special observations one can try to make.

It is interesting to demonstrate to yourself on a night of good "seeing" just how little light-gathering power is needed before an observer can see the planet's distinctive color. (Try your finderscope!) Also interesting is to determine on nights of good "seeing" how much magnification is needed before the globe of Uranus is suspected and how much is needed before it is distinctly visible. Finally, there is a thrill in finding just how high a magnification you can use on this planet before your image degrades—to see a world almost 2 billion miles away as a disk of respectable size on some night of superbly calm atmosphere.

And what of looking for detail in the clouds of Uranus? When Voyager 2 passed the planet in January of 1986, the spacecraft discovered that the clouds of Uranus were virtually featureless. The solar radiation reaching Uranus is far less than that received by Saturn, and the planet's internal heat is less, too. There is thus far less hope of any activity in the atmosphere being vigorous enough to break through the high haze layer. Might Uranus sometimes be more active than it was when Voyager passed? An extremely high-resolution photo taken by a balloon-borne telescope in 1970 showed no detail on Uranus. Of course, there have been a few reports of detail suspected over the years by expert observers, who may have been right.

The color of Uranus is due to the presence of methane. An interesting project would be to compare this color with the hue of Neptune. Since the latter is over 2 magnitudes dimmer than Uranus, however, you would have to compensate for this difference. In 1993, there will come the first chance in history to see Uranus and Neptune in conjunction with each other (the last time this happened was many years before the 1846 discovery of Neptune). The separation will be only about 1°.

How do you find Uranus? Positions for it are given monthly in the popular astronomy magazines, and Uranus moves so slowly that it progresses only a few degrees in the sky each year. During most of the 1990s, it will be continuing to cross the constellation Sagittarius. Uranus has a revolution period of 84 years; it takes an entire long human lifetime for it to circle the whole zodiac.

Conjunctions of Uranus with stars of similar brightness, which happen frequently, make brightness estimates of the planet possible. For decades, the official publications (like the *Astronomical Almanac,* which used to be published as the *American Ephermeris and Nautical Almanac*) were giving values for the magnitudes of the planets based on formulas that were in some cases significantly in error. In the case of Uranus, the predictions had it several tenths of a magnitude fainter than it really is. The new formula is better, but an observer can still try his or her eye at making a magnitude estimate of Uranus (its roughly magnitude 5½ brightness varies a little during the year and will fade a bit as it moves out to its aphelion in 2009). Conjunctions of Uranus and stars are attractive in their own right.

Once in a great many years, Uranus passes in front of a star as seen from at least part of the Earth. Back in 1977, just such an event enabled astronomers to discover the rings of Uranus as these dark and comparatively meager structures occulted a star one by one. Whenever a star gets rather close to Uranus, there is a chance that an undiscovered ring or moon might be identified in the same manner.

Of course, we can trust that Voyager 2 turned up most of what was left to find in the way of satellites and rings at Uranus. Voyager added ten new moons to the already-known five. The tradition of naming them after Shakespearean characters (all but one of the original five had been so named) was continued, so this acting company of moons now includes Juliet, Ophelia, Desdemona, and Cordelia. But can amateur astronomers hope to see any of this satellite play?

The outermost of the original five, Titania and Oberon, are also the largest. Titania is 1,000 miles (1,610 km) across; Oberon, 965 miles (1,550 km). Neither is highly reflective (their albedos are, respectively, 0.28 and 0.24), but both have been seen in telescopes with apertures as small as 6 inches. Both Titania and Oberon are farther from Uranus than the Moon is from Earth, which translates to their being separated by more than 30 arc-seconds from Uranus when they are at greatest elongation from it. See Figure 26. The interesting thing is that in the 1990s these moons will always be fairly near greatest elongation. Is it because their orbits are highly inclined to the equatorial plane of Uranus? No, the reason that they are currently describing nearly circular paths as seen projected onto Earth's sky (their orbits are like the circles on a target with Uranus at the center as the bull's-eye) is far stranger. It is that one of the poles of Uranus is now pointing nearly toward Earth, and the reason for this is that Uranus has its axis almost right in the plane of its orbit. In other words, Uranus is on its side, rolling around its orbit! Any moon of Uranus goes around it not like a horse on a merry-go-round, but like a car on a Ferris wheel.

No one knows why Uranus has such a strange rotation, but it is as-

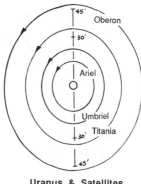

Uranus & Satellites

Figure 26 Orbits of Observable Uranian Satellites. Orientations are only approximate for the early 1990s.

sumed that some cataclysmic event must have knocked it over. Certainly its moons show signs of having been badly damaged. In fact, Miranda, the moon with the 12-mile-high (20-km-high) cliffs, is believed to have been completely broken and reassembled.

The moons of Uranus other than Titania and Oberon are smaller and much closer to the planet so that even having them constantly near their greatest elongation from the planet is not enough help in finding them. Even with a large telescope, an occulting bar (or hair) in the eyepiece would be needed to glimpse them. And, a pole of Uranus really points exactly at Earth and the Sun only twice in the course of the planet's 84-year orbit. A pole of Uranus was last pointed exactly at us in 1985. By 2006, we will be seeing the equator pointed toward us and the moons shuttling straight up and straight down from the planet as seen from Earth.

To confirm the identity of any point of light you think is a moon of Uranus, you must sketch its position and then go back and do the same thing a few nights later. No longer time is required to show the strange motion of one of these moons.

Questions

1. How much light-gathering power do you need to see the color of Uranus? How much magnification do you need to suspect and then to see distinctly its globe? What is the highest magnification you can ever use effectively on Uranus with a given telescope? Do you ever suspect (unlikely as it may be) that you are seeing any detail on the globe?

2. How does the color of Uranus compare with that of Neptune? Compared with that of various stars it passes by? What is your estimate of the brightness of the planet when it passes by stars of similar (and known) brightness? Do you ever get a chance to watch the planet's very close passage of a star for the remote possibility of seeing the star occulted by an unknown ring or moon of Uranus?

3. Can you spot the moons Titania and Oberon? Can you follow part of their odd path in the sky?

46.

Neptune and Triton

Discover how large a telescope is needed to see color in Neptune and how large a magnification is needed to detect its disk. Compare its color with that of stars it passes and with that of Uranus. Keep looking for any possible hint of detail on the planet if you can use high enough magnification to have even a remote chance of seeing a feature. Look for Triton and attempt to track its retrograde orbiting.

In 1846, Neptune became the first planet ever discovered as the result of mathematical calculations. Actually, the story is far more complex than that, and it is a fascinating one (for a thorough account, see Mark Littmann's superb book *Planets Beyond* published by John Wiley & Sons in 1990). In the century and a half since it was first seen knowingly (Galileo did so unknowingly!), we learned most of what we now know about it in 1989. That was when Voyager 2 passed the planet and its amazing moon Triton, showing that Neptune was surprisingly different from Uranus and that Triton was surprisingly different from anything we had ever seen.

For the earthbound observer, Neptune is an object little brighter than magnitude 8 and little larger than 2 arc-seconds across. A night of decent "seeing" and a telescope of at least 4-inch aperture are needed to see its globe. You are looking at a world that is 4 times as wide as Earth but that is over 2½ billion miles away from Earth and the Sun. As many schoolchildren know, Neptune is currently the most distant planet (a distinction that it will return to Pluto in 1999).

Most of the projects that applied to Uranus can be tried on Neptune but carry much greater difficulty. You can learn how large a telescope is needed to see any trace of color in it. Note that the faintest stars in which anyone can glimpse color with the naked eye are about 2nd magnitude and this suggests that to see any hue in Neptune would require a telescope that has a limiting magnitude of at least 13 to 14. Thus, a 6-inch telescope may be necessary.

You can also find what the minimum magnification required is to detect the tiny disk of Neptune on nights of good and nights of very good "seeing." You will find this magnification to be always higher than that with which you can easily scan for Neptune (as is not the case with Uranus). You really must know the position of Neptune exactly and preferably have a finder chart identifying the sometimes numerous stars of similar brightness nearby.

In the next few years, Uranus will be catching up with Neptune and become an increasingly useful guide to it. Not until their conjunction in 1993, however, will they pull to within even a fairly low magnification view of each other. Since Neptune takes 165 years to complete one orbit, it will not return to where it was discovered until 2011. You can count on its being in Sagittarius for many more years to come but, unfortunately, low in the sky for viewers at mid-northern latitudes.

Although Voyager 2 found six new satellites of Neptune, these six and one of the two previously known moons are too small to be bright enough for amateur telescopes. Neptune's other moon, Triton, is quite a different story, however.

Voyager 2 showed that Triton was more reflective and therefore somewhat smaller than had been thought as judged from its brightness. Nevertheless, Triton is not too greatly smaller than Earth's Moon, and its magnitude is about 13. The brightness of Neptune is not too much of a problem when Triton is near its greatest elongation of about 17 arc-seconds (the true distance of Triton from Neptune is about the same as the Moon from Earth). See Figure 27. All things considered, Triton is a little easier to see than any of the moons of Uranus even though it is almost a billion miles farther from us.

What an exciting satellite it is! Voyager 2 showed it to have a strange mixture of terrains, including areas as reflective as anything ever seen in the solar system and other areas that look extremely much like the surface of a cantaloupe. We learned that volcanic eruptions—of liquid nitrogen—were going on even as the spacecraft passed. Scientists now believe that Triton may be a good indication of what Pluto will look like—they are even about the same size and, for now, almost the same distance from the Sun. Triton is the only large moon with a retrograde orbit, and this has

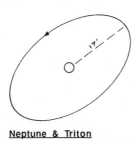

Neptune & Triton

Figure 27 Orbit of Triton. Orientation is only approximate for the early 1990s.

long fired speculation that it was part of some cataclysm that involved Pluto. Voyager 2's information has inspired the speculation not that Pluto was once a moon of Neptune, but that Triton once was not.

You might think there is positively no chance of seeing any surface detail on Neptune. Actually, the chance is probably better than it is with Uranus. Voyager 2 found a surprising amount of activity, including the now-famous Great Dark Spot. How could this be if Neptune is much farther out than blank-faced Uranus? Despite the fact that these planets are nearly twins in size, we can only assume that the mechanism for getting heat from the interior of Neptune is far more efficient than that of Uranus.

Did I say there was a better chance of seeing detail on Neptune than on Uranus? I should have added, if you have a very large telescope and try on numerous nights of excellent "seeing." The problem is that a very high magnification is needed. Remember, even the tiny disk of Uranus appears almost twice as large as that of Neptune.

Questions

1. How large a telescope is needed to see the color of Neptune? How does the color compare with that of Uranus and nearby stars? How low a magnification is enough to reveal the disk of Neptune? What is the highest effective magnification you can ever use on it with your telescope? Do you ever even imagine you are glimpsing some surface detail on Neptune?

2. Can you detect Neptune's large and strange moon Triton? Can you track it for a number of nights and detect its retrograde orbiting?

47.

Pluto

Identify Pluto on several nights to be certain you are looking at the correct object. Try to find out what is the smallest aperture with which you can see Pluto and also the lowest magnification (with a given telescope) that keeps the sky background dark enough to see the planet. With a large telescope and suitable comparison stars, determine whether you can detect any of Pluto's brightness variations.

Any pair of binoculars is capable of showing Neptune. But even when Pluto is brightest, it is 200 times dimmer than Neptune. When both are at opposition, the disk of Neptune appears about 20 times smaller in apparent diameter than that of Jupiter, requiring a medium-sized telescope to glimpse. Even when Pluto is largest, it appears 20 times smaller than Neptune! It is by far the smallest planet in true size and considerably smaller than Earth's Moon. Even the largest telescopes in the world have not quite been able to show Pluto's disk.

Pluto is almost a byword for the farthest, coldest, and most mysterious. Actually, between 1979 and 1999, the planet is not quite as far from the Sun as Neptune. This is because Pluto's distance from the Sun varies tremendously and we have had the privilege of being alive in the time of its perihelion, 1989. Its distance from the Sun and Earth now is only about 60 percent of the aphelion distance it achieved in 1866. No planet has an orbit that departs anywhere near so far from circularity. Neither does any planet come close to matching the orbital inclination of 17°, an inclination that sends Pluto sometimes far outside the zodiac constellations in which we always see the other planets, the Sun, and the Moon. But it is the size of Pluto's orbit that amazes most. These 20 years during which it is closer than Neptune represent less than one-twelfth its full journey of 247½ years to circle the Sun.

The statistics about Pluto are overwhelming. Yet, there really are a few observing projects that amateur astronomers can try with Pluto.

Of course, most observers are happy just to have seen Pluto. The telescope size recommended is usually at least 10 inches. In skies less than excellently dark, this advice is wise. But a few people have seen Pluto in a 6-inch telescope, and at least one person with even less aperture. If my memory doesn't fail me, that person is none other than Pluto's discoverer, the marvelous Clyde Tombaugh. The story of Tombaugh's discovery of Pluto as a youth in 1930 is an inspiring story. And into his eighties,

Tombaugh has seemed to have carried with him the strong zest for observing that marks the true amateur spirit in astronomy—the spirit of the individual who, whether he or she earns a living by astronomy or not, is in love with the subject.

To identify Pluto will require an excellent finder chart. Guy Ottewell's *Astronomical Calendar* includes one each year, as do the January issues of *Sky & Telescope* and *Astronomy* magazines. Use a fairly high magnification in order to reduce the brightness of the sky background relative to the point of light that is Pluto. Now, see whether you can detect this point. Even if you think you have an object in the right position, the confirmation that you have seen Pluto should really be made on a second night. Has the speck moved right to the new position where it should be if it really is Pluto?

If there is anything more that amateurs can do than just find Pluto, it must be to study its brightest variations. These variations occur with a period of 6.39 days, which we know to be Pluto's rotation period (hence the variations must be caused by more and less reflective areas of Pluto's surface being presented to us). Are the variations large enough to be detected by an amateur astronomer with a large telescope and good comparison stars? (By the way, Pluto is apparently a little dimmer than the magnitude 13.6 that one usually sees listed for these near-perihelion years—no doubt because we are now seeing more of darker equatorial regions than we did when the formula for Pluto was written many years ago.)

Repeatedly during a period of a few years in every 124 (half of Pluto's revolution period), Pluto dims by up to half a magnitude for another reason. The disk of its moon, darker than itself, is passing in front of it as seen from Earth. See Figure 28.

Pluto's moon, Charon, was discovered in 1977 and came as one of the great surprises of planetary astronomy. The smallest planet, which some doubted was really more than an escaped moon of Neptune, had a moon of its own—and not just any moon. Charon is over half as wide as Pluto, is located only 12,400 miles (20,000 km) from it, and is tidally locked with Pluto in a unique way . . . *both* planet and moon always keep the same face toward each other. The discovery of Charon—a mere bump on images of Pluto—enabled astronomers to figure out numerous important properties of Pluto (including the fact that, like Uranus, Pluto has its axis of rotation almost right in the plane of its orbit). And what good fortune that Charon was not found too many years later. The very enlightening series of Pluto–Charon eclipses lasted from 1985 until 1990. At their most extreme, these events must have been detectable by large amateur telescopes. Did any amateur astronomers observe them? Our next chance will not come along until the twenty-second century!

Figure 28 Charon as Seen from Pluto.

Questions

1. Can you find Pluto on one night and then verify your finding by locating it in a different place a few nights later? What is the smallest aperture with which you can see Pluto? The lowest magnification with which the sky background is dark enough to see it through your particular telescope?

2. With a large telescope and knowledge of the approximate brightness of nearby comparison stars, can you detect any of the brightness variations of Pluto?

COMETS, ASTEROIDS, AND METEORS

48.

General Observations of Comets

Observe as many comets as you can each year, with as many different optical instruments as you can. Observe as much of each apparition as possible. Identify the coma and, if visible, any tail. Make sketches at low magnification showing the inner and the outer coma. Make sketches at higher magnifications showing finer detail in the inner coma (and tail), if any is detectable.

Nothing in the sky has stirred more terror throughout history than comets. They could appear unexpectedly anywhere in the sky and at any time. They could move in novel paths and sometimes with a week-to-week or night-to-night speed alarmingly greater than that of the planets. The form and brightness of comets were the most frightening aspects of all. Each lifetime, a few comets could rival or surpass even the brightest planets and have their heads grow enormous—a fuzzy patch of light bigger than the Moon—and sprout shining tails so immense they would span a large section of the sky. See Figure 29.

People in the distant past believed that comets were omens, usually evil ones. People in the more recent past feared that these vast astronomical objects would collide with Earth, causing even greater disaster—perhaps the end of life on our world. Today, we believe that comets occasionally do collide with Earth and, in fact, that such a collision may have led to the destruction of the dinosaurs and much other life on Earth many millions of years ago. But the phrase "millions of years" is the key: there is no evidence that major devastation of our planet by comets should happen at intervals of less than millions of years. And there continues to be scientific speculation that comet impacts in the early solar system may have helped form Earth's oceans and played a crucial role in preparing the way for life on our planet. Comets may be both great givers and takers of life.

Even today, comets remain the most mysterious type of object in our solar system. Comets also remain more apt to having important secrets unlocked from them by amateur observers than probably any other celestial body. There are a number of reasons why amateurs' contributions to understanding comets can be so great.

First of all, the fact that previously unknown comets can suddenly become bright enough to see at any time or any place in the sky means that amateurs will sometimes be the first to spot them—and that even afterward the new object may be difficult to fit into professional observing schedules

Figure 29 Comet West.

(often planned long in advance). Often, comets are at their most interesting when they are low in a twilight sky—a difficult situation for most observatory telescopes and much of their instrumentation but not for amateur observers with portable telescopes and trained eyes. Comets can change so rapidly that constant surveillance is needed if some of their key activity is not to be missed. Once again, it is amateurs in their great numbers around the world who can perform this function when the great observatories of the world are clouded over or must be otherwise occupied.

The amateur astronomer with a 6-inch telescope is likely to have somewhere between about two and six comets become bright enough to detect each year. A larger telescope will reveal more. Admittedly, a rough average of only about one comet each year may get close to, or surpass, the naked-eye limit. Most of the comets that a dedicated observer will see appear as very faint patches of light, often without sign of even the famous comet trademark, a tail. But these are still novel, moving, changing objects about which some vital facts can be learned—possibly on some nights by no one else in the world so well as one ambitious amateur observer. And even the dimmer comets are a preparation in observing practice for their far greater kin which will blaze with amazingly intricate detail in an observer's sky a few times a decade.

What is a comet? We now know that Fred Whipple was essentially correct in 1950 when he wrote that the heart of a comet, its *nucleus*, must be a kind of mountain of ice, usually just a few miles across, in which various frozen gases and dust were trapped. There might or might not be a solid rocky core within this ice. When a comet gets close enough to the Sun—say, inward of or near to the orbit of Mars—the solar radiation heats the surface ice, causing it, in the vacuum of space, not to melt (go from a solid to a liquid) but rather to *sublime* (go directly from a solid to a gas or vapor). Soon, the astronomically small nucleus is surrounding itself with a cloud of (sometimes quite dusty) gas (mostly water vapor but also many other ingredients). The cloud grows to a visible size that rivals that of the largest planets and often surpasses them greatly. This cloud, because of its ill-defined, fuzzy appearance, is called the *coma* (Latin for "hair"). The term *comet* is from the Latin for "long-haired one" (the thought here is of the tail streaming out from the head like long locks of hair). The nucleus—too shrouded and too small to see—and the coma together form the *head* of the comet. Whether a particular comet produces a visible *tail*—a streamer or fan of gas and/or dust driven out in the direction opposite the Sun—depends on several factors, including its size and how close it comes to Earth and the Sun.

When you look for a comet, you will find that it appears brightest and can be seen to extend over the largest area when you use low magnification. Sometimes, a smaller telescope is actually advantageous for looking at a comet if you can use a much lower magnification than with another telescope. The reason that this is true of comets and really of no other solar system bodies is that comets are extended objects. You are looking at something more like a patch of thin fog than a solid globe (even though we see only the cloud features of some planets, we are looking at the tops of very thick cloud-layers). There is no definite outer edge to the coma or to a comet tail; the gases just get thinner and thinner. The more you magnify, the more you spread out the available illumination from these gases over a larger apparent area—you reduce the surface brightness too much and are able to perceive less and less of the outer coma.

Of course, if there is any structure at all to be seen in the inner coma, you will want to use more magnification to make it appear large enough to study. Thus, the procedure with a "typical" comet is to (1) find it with low magnification and sketch this view of the largest amount of coma you can and tail you can and (2) then try somewhat higher magnification to determine whether there is any structure in the brightest parts that you can make out and sketch. If you are a novice comet-watcher, you will want to familiarize yourself with the various appearances of the coma and tail (and they do vary greatly, both from comet to comet and over the course of one comet's apparition). If you are a more experienced observer, you should remind yourself to use as many different magnifications—indeed, as many different eyepieces, even those giving the same magnification—as are available. Study the question of how little and how much magnification with different eyepieces and telescopes is advantageous for viewing various kinds of comets at each stage of their apparitions.

If many comets are new and unexpected, how do you find out about them in time to observe them?

That's a good question. The popular astronomy magazines finalize their text several months before a given issue appears, increasing the possibility that they might not be able to tell you about a certain comet until it is already past its prime. One solution is to call *Sky & Telescope* magazine's "Skyline" phone message (see the "Sources of Information" section). Usually each Friday (sometimes more often), the several-minutes-long recorded message is updated. It gives the latest news on astronomy and space discoveries—including the discovery of any comet likely to be accessible to most amateur telescopes—and the latest observing prospects, including the positions for any currently interesting comets. The ultimate source for news on comet discoveries is *IAU (International Astronomical Union) Circulars*, but these are rather expensive to subscribe to (a standard subscription includes many circulars that are about objects like X-ray sources, which only professional astronomers can hope to study). Is there an extra option to "Skyline" for the person who wants finder charts and information on somewhat dimmer comets and wants it quickly and cheaply? Yes, there are various amateur astronomers who use IAU circulars and personal computers to run their own "news services." One of these that I would recommend for comets is the CRAS or Comet Rapid Announcement Service (see the "Sources of Information" section).

One final question: might you discover a new comet yourself? Yes, many are found by amateurs with small telescopes. Because the search for new comets requires considerable knowledge, experience, and patience, however, try it only *after* you have practiced the comet projects of this book. (Then, for tips on how to search for and report a new comet, see Phil Harrington's *Touring the Universe through Binoculars*.)

Questions

1. How many comets can you glimpse with telescopes of different apertures this year? How much of each apparition can you observe?

2. Can you identify both a coma and a tail on the comet you observe? What is the comet's appearance and approximate size in your sketch made with low magnification? What finer structure in the brightest parts, if any, is visible in your sketches done with higher magnification? What magnification proves to be the highest useful?

49.

Short-Period and Long-Period Comets

Observe as many short-period (periodic) comets and long-period comets as you can each year. In a fairly bright periodic comet, look especially for the possibility of a sunward fan and a narrow, straight gas tail. Compare the comet's brightness and when it does or does not brighten in accordance with predictions based on its behavior at past returns. In a fairly bright long-period comet, look for much detail in the inner coma and the presence of perhaps both dust tail and gas tail. Compare the comet's performance to predictions, noting how different it may be.

Even in making very elementary observations of comets, it is valuable to know a little about the major different kinds of comets and comet tails. The most important categorization of comets is into *short-period*, or *periodic*, comets and *long-period* comets.

Periodic comets are those that return to the inner solar system frequently enough to be observed repeatedly in history or even in a human lifetime. Most of the periodics have orbits that take between only about 3 and 20 years to complete. A few, like Halley's, require something closer to the whole length of a human lifetime or even longer. The somewhat arbitrary but useful cutoff point is 200 years. Any comet that takes longer than this to return to the end of its orbit where the Sun warms it enough to become visible (depending on how close to Earth it comes) is considered a long-period comet. We can compute that some long-period comets have orbits that take thousands or even millions of years to complete!

If you did not know before, you may have just reasoned that comets must travel on orbits that are greatly elongated ellipses. How else could a comet only be near enough to the Sun and Earth to be visible for a small part of its orbit and invisible for the rest if the rest of the orbit did not take it out—perhaps far out—from the inner solar system? If this is what you figured, you are right. When Edmund Halley performed his calculations, he discovered that observations of a bright comet roughly every 75 years could be explained by assuming this was one object in a cigar-shaped orbit with one end within the orbit of Venus and the other end beyond the orbit of Neptune. Figure 30 shows an *elliptical* orbit and also a nearly *parabolic* orbit. The latter is the kind of orbit a long-period comet has because its ellipse is greatly elongated (we get to observe only a little part of the orbit near the sunward end, and this part is virtually identical to that of a comet of much shorter period). The outline of the third kind of comet orbit, a *hyperbolic* orbit, is the kind that a comet's path would travel if it were from another solar system and merely curving around our Sun once before hurtling back out into interstellar space. No comet that has yet had its orbit determined has been found to have entered ʌʋr solar system on a hyperbolic orbit.

Since each passage by the Sun uses up more of a comet's ice, we know that there must be a fresh source of comets from which our supply gets replenished. In the year of Fred Whipple's theory about the composition of comets (1950), Jan Oort proposed that all comets originally come from a

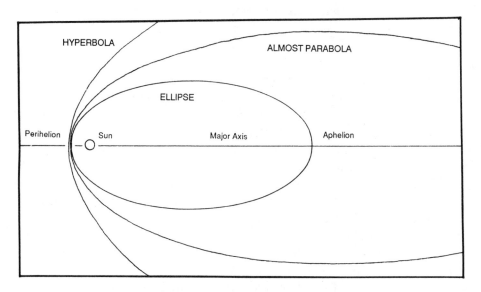

HYPERBOLA   ALMOST PARABOLA

ELLIPSE

Perihelion   Sun   Major Axis   Aphelion

Figure 30 Different Shapes of Comet Orbits.

vast shell of at least millions of billions of comets far out beyond the orbits of the most distant planets. The scenario would be that, when a star other than our Sun passed rather near our solar system, it would disrupt many of the virgin comets in this *Oort cloud*, speeding up some, slowing down others, and succeeding in sending some of them plunging inward for thousands of years until they curved around the Sun in a new, greatly elongated orbit—the orbit of a long-period comet. The reasoning would be that after several returns such a comet would pass close enough to a planet (usually Jupiter) to have its orbit altered yet again. This time it would have its aphelion near the orbit of Jupiter (or Saturn or Uranus or Neptune), and thus its orbit would be far less elongated—the orbit of a periodic (short-period) comet.

Whether or not there are several zones to the Oort cloud, inner and outer, and whether or not comets originally formed near the orbits of Uranus and Neptune before being kicked out to the Oort cloud, we do not know. But the basic idea of the Oort cloud, however, remains the accepted explanation for where comets come from.

For the observer, there are profound differences to expect in the appearance of periodic versus long-period comets.

The periodic comets almost all tend to be intrinsically dim and show relatively less activity. Many of them seldom, if ever, produce a tail or at least one that is visible from Earth. That this should be the case is not sur-

171

prising, considering that many of the periodics must have already weathered hundreds of passages by the Sun.

The long-period comets are not all intrinsically bright, but some of them are. In fact, if an intrinsically bright long-period comet passes near the Sun and/or Earth, what can result is not just a naked-eye comet but a brilliant display, rivaling the brightest stars and planets. A coma so bright will have dramatic sharp structures of various kinds (see Activity 51), and such a comet is almost certain to produce a major tail. The longest and most favorably angled of these tails have stretched as long as halfway and even more than halfway across the sky.

By no means do all long-period comets put on great displays, and Halley's Comet is the prime example of a periodic comet that does at some returns put on a sensational show. Note that Halley's Comet returns to the vicinity of the Sun far less often than a comet like Comet Encke, which has a period of only 3.3 years (the shortest known), and thus its expected lifetime as a bright object is much longer.

The advantage of short-period comets is that we know more of what to expect from them and can be prepared. Also, if the period is short enough, we can learn more about our old friends a number of times in our life. The advantage of long-period comets is their potential for greater brightness and greater activity—we never get to see them come back again, but while they are here they may be bright enough to display many features that can enlighten us about the nature of comets.

If your target is a fairly bright short-period comet, look for a sunward fan of light that the coma sometimes displays. On the other hand, since some of these comets have little left but gas, look very carefully for a very faint, thin streamer of gas tail. For this and other attempts to observe very dim features in comets (or dim comets themselves), you will want to use the technique of *averted vision*—that is, directing your gaze slightly to one side of where you really want to look, thereby getting the light to fall on the part of your retina that is most sensitive to dim light. Some of these periodic comets have a well-established tendency to be dramatically brighter either a certain amount of time after perihelion or a certain amount of time before perihelion. Therefore, read up on them in the astronomy magazines or, most dependably, in the huge "Comets" section of Guy Ottewell's *Astronomical Calendar* each year.

If your target is a long-period comet, it will be a new one and there will be no information to read about past returns. But you can hope that it will become brighter than almost any of the periodics and, if so, capable of showing far more structure in both the inner coma and the tail. The long-period comets are more likely (but not certain) to display more of a dust tail—broader, fuzzier, usually easier to see than a gas tail. A long-period comet, especially if it passes fairly close to the Sun (say, within the orbit of Venus), is likely to be brighter after perihelion than before.

The following two activities deal in greater detail with coma structures, the different kinds of tail, and the brightness behavior of comets.

Questions

1. Are you observing a periodic or a long-period comet? (Occasionally, a new periodic is discovered; so you may have to guess for yourself what type you are looking at.) How many of each kind can you observe in a year?

2. What features of the periodic comet's coma can be seen? Is any tail present? If so, is it one of gas? If you have read how bright and active or how long-tailed the periodic you are seeing has been at past returns, how does this return seem to compare—both as predicted and as you really see it? If the comet is predicted to undergo an intrinsic brightening a certain number of weeks before or after perihelion, can you confirm that it does?

3. What features of a long-period comet's coma can be seen? Is any dust tail present? If so, can you also see a gas tail? How does the comet perform compared to predictions? Is its intrinsic brightness greater after perihelion?

50.

The Brightness of Comets

Estimate the brightness of a comet compared to nearby stars by your method of choice (Sidgwick, Bobrovnikoff, Morris, or Beyer). Experiment with seeing how different your values are derived from using the four different methods. Study how much difference there is in the values from magnitude estimates of the same comet with different apertures. See whether you can detect any delta effect in the brightness of a diffuse comet passing near Earth.

The brightness of comets is notoriously difficult to predict. Unlike planets or stars, comets shine by both reflected and emitted light. The emitted light is the fluorescence of certain gases under the influence of solar radiation and the solar wind (outflow of atomic particles from the Sun). Part of the standard magnitude formula for comets is a term for the comet's distance from the Sun, and part is a term for its distance from the Earth. But the amount of coma there is to reflect light and the amount of gas there is to fluoresce are highly variable—depending ultimately in part on freaks of activity in the melting (or, rather, subliming) of a comet nucleus (which may be displaying inactive dusty or very active icy areas to the Sun depending on intricacies of its orbit and its rotation). Therefore, every comet ends up being given its own distinctive *absolute magnitude*—that is, the brightness it would be if it were 1 AU (astronomical unit, the average Sun–Earth distance) from both the Sun and Earth—and its own distinctive *n*, or brightening, factor—that is, how rapidly its magnitude varies as a function of decreasing or increasing distance from the Sun. The brightness behavior of many comets is so complex that even all this is not enough. To get a formula that predicts their brightness requires assigning them different absolute magnitudes for different parts of their apparitions and sometimes a variable *n*.

Trying to calculate how bright a new comet will get is fascinating, but here we will concentrate on the equally interesting outdoors task of observing comets and trying to estimate their magnitudes. Reliable magnitude estimates can greatly reduce the difficulties of the calculator.

The four methods of estimating comet brightness all try to get around the difficulty of comparing the brightness of an extended object to that of point sources—the stars near the comet. The methods are as follows:

1. *Sidgwick Method (In–Out)*. Memorize the appearance of the in-focus comet and compare it to stars placed out of focus until their blurred images attain a state similar to that which the in-focus comet had.

2. *Bobrovnikoff Method (Out–Out)*. Place both comet and stars out of focus until they are nearly the same size and then compare their brightnesses.

3. *Morris Method*. Memorize the slightly out-of-focus image of the comet and then compare it to out-of-focus images of the stars when they become the same size as the memorized image of the comet.

4. *Beyer Method*. Set both comet and stars more and more out of

focus until they disappear and then compare their brightnesses according to the order and timing of their disappearances.

Much can be said about the advantages and disadvantages of these different methods. Actually, certain ones are better for certain kinds of comets and worse for others. The method that most beginners use, I believe, is the Bobrovnikoff method, and it does have the excellent advantage of requiring no memorization. Many of the more experienced observers prefer the Morris method. Do the methods produce the same results? In the hands (or eyes) of practiced observers, they roughly do (again, depending on the kind of comet—large and diffuse or small and condensed). There is no doubt, however, that even the best observers have some slight personal bias. Some tend to estimate comets brighter than most other observers; some, fainter, even when they are using the same method. Whichever method you choose, be sure to use this one method for the duration of observing a particular comet.

The important things to remember are to practice and, a very basic point: to use the lowest magnification possible. If the comet is bright enough to use the naked eye (magnification 1X), then use the naked eye. Of course, it is interesting to compare the magnitude estimates you get with the naked eye, binoculars (or finderscope), and a telescope on the same comet. Generally, the more diffuse or the larger the apparent size of the comet, the greater the difference in magnitude estimates will be with eye, binoculars, and telescope. Almost invariably, you will find that the lower the magnification, the greater the total brightness of the comet obtained.

A few points must be made about the standard comet brightness formula and its relation to the magnitudes you actually see. The formula produces magnitude predictions for a standard aperture—actually 6.8 cm (2.7 inches)—because this was the average of the various instruments used in a study of the effect of aperture made by Bobrovnikoff in the 1940s. Therefore, if the brightness formula predicts that a comet will reach magnitude 4.5, you can expect that the naked-eye view—the eye having an aperture of less than 6.8 cm—would be brighter than 4.5 and that the view in a 4- or 6-inch telescope—an aperture more than 6.8 cm—would be a little dimmer than 4.5. Of course, the amount of this *aperture effect* depends on the type of comet. A very large, diffuse comet will have a greater amount of outer coma that is perceptible to the naked eye and not to the telescope; thus, it may be very much brighter to the naked eye.

Similar to aperture effect is *delta effect*. The Greek letter delta (Δ) is used as a symbol to represent the comet's distance from Earth (r is the symbol used to represent the comet's distance from the Sun). Having a comet come closer to Earth is like magnifying our view of it. If a comet comes close enough to Earth, even its naked-eye brightness might fall a little behind predictions because its coma would be spread over so large an area that the outer portions would have too low a surface brightness to perceive. In practice, however, this kind of delta effect is seldom a problem. Only a rather diffuse comet that comes quite close to Earth would typically exhibit it.

The final thing to remember about comet brightness is that it is subject to remarkable fluctuations. Besides the "surges" that can happen at certain times before or after perihelion, there are "flares" in comet brightness that are truly remarkable. A small flare would be half a magnitude or so. But some comets have suddenly brightened by up to 10 magnitudes in a brief time! Clearly, comets are objects that deserve steady and long-term surveillance.

Questions

1. How bright do you rate a comet on a certain night using your method of choice (one of the four described in this activity)? How bright using the other methods?

2. How bright is a particular comet when its brightness is estimated with instruments of different aperture? Might the comet you observe exhibit delta effect during the part of its apparition when it passes closest to Earth?

3. Do you detect any surges in brightness (above what would be expected) over a number of weeks? Do you detect any briefer but perhaps much greater flares in brightness?

51.

The Size, Color, and Features of Comets

Measure the diameter of the coma and estimate its degree of condensation. Study its overall shape and see whether it evolves from being amorphous to being fan-shaped or, if bright, having a parabolic outline surrounded by a more circular glow. Note any color visible in the coma. Observe a gas tail, if visible, trying to

detect its color and any structure in it like forks or ion rays.
Estimate the length of the gas tail. Observe a dust tail, noting any
curvature and the position angles of its leading and trailing
edges, as well as those of any brighter branches in it. Note any
color in it. Estimate its length and width. Watch for any trace of
an anti-tail and, if you see one, sketch it nightly and hourly
(noting the time of your sketches) to see how much its length and
shape change.

The two major visible parts of a comet, the coma and the tail, may show marvelous variety. The brighter the comet, the more likely that its activity will produce these structures. Figure 31 shows the structure of a comet, which is the subject of our discussion here.

First, let's study the coma. The truly enormous coma hides within it the comparatively tiny nucleus. But one important task for amateur comet-observers is to determine the coma's apparent size. To do so, you use the lowest suitable magnification that can properly show the coma.

The method for measuring the comet's diameter (which requires no equipment besides your telescope) is the drift method. You time how long it takes for a star near the comet (or for the center of the comet) to drift across the center of your field of view (it will be different at different declinations in the sky). You should already know the angular diameter of your field of view (it can be computed simply by taking the eyepiece's apparent field—say, 50°—and dividing this figure by the magnification—if 100×, then you have a ½°-wide true field of view). Knowing these two things, you need only time how long it takes for the entire width of the coma to pass off the edge of the field and you can then calculate what fraction of the field's angular width the coma's diameter is.

Coma diameters can range from 1 arc-minute (and less) to ½° or even to 1° or more wide. They grow until the comet gets close enough to the Sun for the solar wind to start compressing them.

A coma will show color only if it is bright enough (with medium-sized amateur telescopes, this may mean sixth or fifth magnitude, roughly, depending very much on the particular comet). The most likely color for you to notice is blue from one of the kinds of fluorescing gas. But in a very bright comet, the gold of sunlight reflected by great quantities of dust in the coma may also be seen.

The coma of a rather dim or inactive comet may appear quite amorphous, but a brighter and more active one can show extensions at various position angles. Note which position angle (PA)—north is 0°, east is 90°, and so on through 360° back to north—remembering that objects in your

177

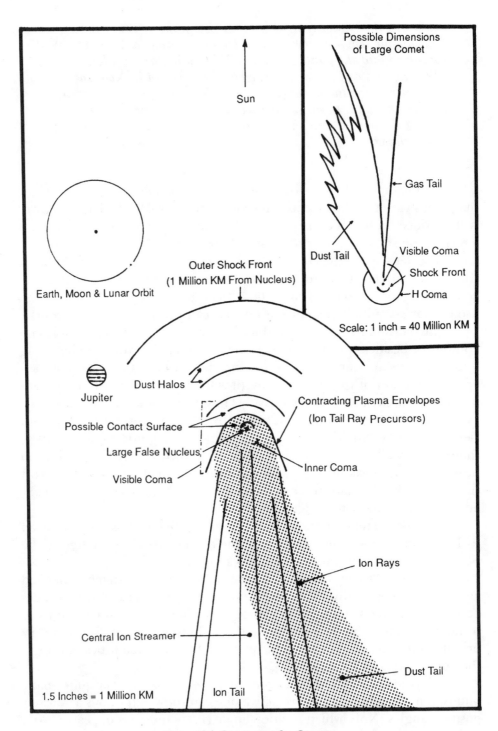

Figure 31 Structure of a Comet.

178

field drift from east to west in counterpoise to Earth's rotation. A still brighter comet, getting quite near the Sun, begins to have its coma or, rather, its ionized gas coma driven back to assume a parabolic outline.

The overall shape of the coma may be harder to define, however, than another property of it—its degree of condensation. How much is the coma condensed toward its center? Table 10 describes a few of the ratings in the 0-to-9 scale.

A very small, intense condensation in the innermost coma is sometimes still called "the nucleus." But this should be referred to as the "apparent nucleus" (or by a better term!) because it is not really the icy center of the comet but rather a dense area of gas and/or dust. Dense? Here is as good a place as any to remind ourselves that comets, though huge, are incredibly tenuous. You will see stars shining through an inner coma sometimes. A million-mile-wide visible coma could come from the top few inches of just parts of a few-mile-wide nucleus. And what of the famous statement about the still more tenuous tail? That a million miles of it could be packed into a single suitcase.

In addition to the so-called apparent nucleus, a bright comet may display various sunward-pointing features such as large "fans," "envelopes" or "halos" (expanding outward from the central coma), and smaller projections (requiring high magnification) known as "jets." Many of these you will only see on those rare occasions when you have a truly spectacular comet in your view. The important thing, once again, is to practice, sketching what is seen (and nothing more!) in each coma you get to observe, even if it is a tenth-magnitude puff on the edge of vision.

Many of the fainter comets you see may not even show a tail. Once a tail is sighted, however, you will be spellbound to see whether it grows further and what structure may become visible in it.

There are two different major types of comet tails (both of which can occur with a large, active comet). There is (1) the *gas tail*, which is sometimes called the *ion* or *plasma tail*, and (2) there is the *dust tail*.

Table 10
Degree of Condensation in Comas, on a 0-to-9 Scale

Deg. Cond.	Description
0	Diffuse coma with uniform brightness (no central condensation visible).
3	Diffuse coma with brightness increasing gradually toward center.
6	Coma shows definite intensity peak at center.
9	Coma appears stellar (or, in a few cases, coma develops a sharp edge like that of a planetary disk).

The gas tail is straight, narrow, and blue when any color at all can be glimpsed in it. The difficulty of seeing it lies in the fact that so much of its light is in wavelengths at the violet end of the spectrum where our eyes are not very sensitive. Photography with typical film shows gas tails better than we see them. Nevertheless, there have been cases of gas tails traceable for many degrees and showing their internal structure rather readily. The structure is *ion rays*, which in a major comet keep forming and then collapsing into a central ray much like the metal rods of an umbrella when you collapse it. I recall vividly my views of a number of these rays in the fifth magnitude Halley's Comet in December of 1985. Far more difficult to glimpse visually most of the time must be the amazing DEs, or disconnection events, in which the gas tail becomes detached and is immediately replaced by the stub of a new one.

The reason a gas tail is straight, pointing almost exactly straight away from the Sun, is that its ionized atomic particles can be carried off at tremendous speeds by the charged particles of the solar wind.

Dust tails are different and show it by their shape, which is broad and curved. The particles of dust, though mostly extremely small, are moved—far less rapidly than gas atoms and molecules are by the solar wind—by the radiation pressure of sunlight. (It seems hard for us to credit sunlight with such pressure, but in the frictionless vacuum of space its effect on tiny dust particles is significant.) Since the comet is moving onward while the dust from it gets pushed off by sunlight, the dust lags behind the comet, forming a broad arc in which the position of a particle is a measure of how large (or rather how large and light-colored, thus pushable by sunlight) it is and when it was released from the comet. In rare cases, like that of 1976's Comet West, we see the dust tail fairly face-on so that interior structure is visible and so that the dust tail appears completely separate (completely to one side) of the gas tail.

This situation is usually not the case, however. More often, we are closer to being in the plane of the comet's orbit and seeing the gas tail and dust tail superimposed from what is more like an edge-on view. Thus, the dust tail, which may appear golden in very bright, dusty comets, usually seems at least partly to blend with the gas tail.

The biggest question about a comet's tail is, of course, how long is it? The naked eye can perform great feats in seeing the faintest extensions of a very bright comet's tail. But with most comets, including slightly less bright ones, the tail may be too dim to see without optical aid. Use the known width of your field of view or the known distance between two stars to estimate the tail's length. Are there several different parts of a gas or dust tail to measure? If so, make sure you record the position angle in which each is located.

180

Finally, one more type of comet tail must be mentioned. Occasionally, a comet may have a tail whose position angle shows it to be pointing back toward the Sun—a seeming impossibility. The explanation for this *anti-tail* is in the viewing angle. If large particles in a dust tail lag far enough behind a comet's head and we get to see an edgewise view (looking right along the plane of the comet's orbit and thus the plane of the dust tail), then we can sometimes see past the head to this part of the dust tail, making the tail seem as though it were pointing sunward. Such sights are seldom visible for more than a few days and should be studied carefully, for much about the true physical composition of the dust may be learned from them. We do know this about the dust of comet tails: Some of it ends up making a second and dramatic appearance perhaps thousands of years later . . . when it enters our atmosphere to burn up as a meteor in one of our familiar yearly meteor showers.

Questions

1. What is the angular size of the coma you observe? What is its degree of condensation? Do you note any blue or gold color in it if it is rather bright?

2. Do you observe an apparent nucleus? What about sunward fans? Or jets? Or envelopes or halos? Is the overall form of the coma amorphous, roughly circular, or fan-shaped? Or does it, in a bright comet, have the outline of a parabola (the coma of ionized gas) surrounded by a glow (the coma of dust)?

3. Do you observe a gas tail? Can you detect its color visually? Can you see any splits in it or smaller structure like ion rays? How long is the gas tail?

4. Do you observe a dust tail? Does it blend with a gas tail? Can you detect a distinct curve to it? Does it show any color or any structure (most likely brighter branches in itself)? What position angle are these in? What is the position angle of the leading edge (closest to the gas tail and the *extended radius vector*, which is the straight line from the Sun to the comet's head extended onward still farther away from the Sun)? What is the position angle of the trailing edge? How long is the dust tail?

5. Do you glimpse an anti-tail? How many nights is it visible? How do its form and length on your sketches change during this period?

52.

The Asteroids

Observe the Big Four asteroids, noting the color of the brightest ones, Vesta and Ceres. Try to study the brightness variations of asteroids like Eros. Listen for announcements about the close approach of asteroids and try to see these swift-moving objects. Watch for asteroidal occultations of stars when there is predicted to be a chance of one somewhere in your country or part of your country. Try to identify as many asteroids as you can in one sky, one night, one year—and one lifetime.

There are only nine known major planets, but there are several thousand known *minor planets*. These are the *asteroids*, so called because they appear starlike in telescopes due to their smallness. The largest ones can be more than one-third the diameter of Pluto; the brightest can become brighter than Uranus; the closest have been far from the traditional *asteroid belt* and passed as near as less than half the distance of Earth's own Moon from us.

The asteroids are far less observed than they deserve to be. They represent a remarkable variety of worldlets, whose very presence in the solar system is a mystery, whose natural resources might eventually be of great use, and whose names and stories of discovery are filled with colorful interest.

For a number of years in the 1970s and first half of the 1980s, their great champion was Dr. Jay Gunter, whose free publication "Tonight's Asteroids" was always beautifully written and researched. But the good doctor was wise enough to know that it was time at last to take on new challenges as he entered his own upper seventies. Asteroid-watchers, however, can still hunt up selected asteroids in the astronomy magazines and publications like Guy Ottewell's *Astronomical Calendar* (see the "Sources of Information" section). There are also several special projects to try besides trying to see as many of these little worlds as possible.

The biggest, brightest asteroids actually can be glimpsed with the naked eye at some of their best oppositions. Brightest can be Vesta, which has such a high albedo that it can outshine even the largest of the asteroids, much bigger Ceres. Vesta and Ceres, together with the asteroids Pallas and Juno, are known as "the Big Four," even though we now know that they are neither the four biggest nor the four brightest. They were, however, the first four discovered just after the start of the nineteenth century.

The color of asteroids like Ceres and Vesta can be appreciated even in quite small telescopes. A few others can brighten into the magnitude 7 to 8 range in which color might be glimpsed.

But one thing even some rather faint asteroids display that can be followed is brightness variations. Most famous in this respect is Eros, an asteroid that can come quite close to Earth. Its brightness at an average opposition is about 10.0; its variation in brightness can range from nothing up to as much as 1.5 magnitudes—because of, we may be sure, a highly irregular shape that presents Earth and the Sun with varying amounts of surface. See Figure 32. The period of Eros's variations is 5 hours, 16 minutes, which we may assume is the little world's rotation period. Other asteroids whose brightness varies include Eunomia (average opposition magnitude 8.7; variation 0.4 to 0.5; period 6 hours, 5 minutes), Kleopatra (magnitude 10.0; variation 0.4 to 1.6; period 5 hours, 36 minutes), and Nysa (magnitude 9.9; variation 0.2 to 0.4; period 6 hours, 25 minutes). Spectral studies of asteroids can tell us much about them, and we find that Nysa is one of the rare asteroids of very high albedo (even higher than that of Vesta). The assumption is that these lighter-toned bodies were originally the outside, or upper crust, of whatever body or bodies were the ancestors of the asteroids.

What is the latest thinking on where and what the asteroids originally came from? The idea that a single planet exploded to form them is contradicted by spectral evidence that they seem to derive from not one but a small number of different original worlds—none of which could have been tremendously larger than today's biggest asteroids. Even if there are tens of thousands of asteroids above, say, a mile or so in diameter, the total mass of them would be only a small fraction of that of the Moon. The asteroids may be interesting, but they really are small.

One of the most interesting things about them is that not all of them are confined to orbiting in zones that together make up a so-called asteroid belt between the orbits of Mars and Jupiter. Long-term gravitational perturbations of some of the belt asteroids eventually can kick them out on orbits that swoop right across those of Mars, Earth, Venus, and even Mercury. Asteroids can hit Earth. One of them, rather than a comet, may have been the celestial source of the dinosaurs' demise. In our own century, quite a few asteroids have come within a few million miles of Earth, and one in 1991 to less than half the Moon's distance from Earth. To observe one of these close-passing Apollo asteroids is thrilling. The motion may be fast enough to be detectable at high magnification, zooming it most of the way around the heavens in one day. But sometimes we have very brief advance warning. Your most likely chance to hear about the close approach and get positions for the asteroid in time would probably

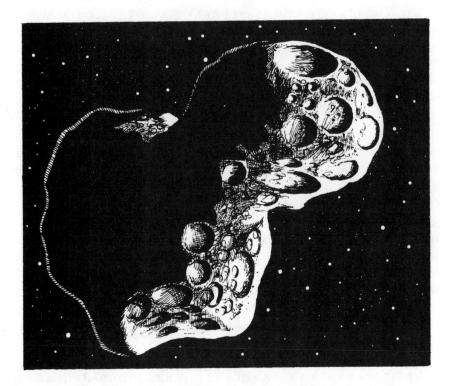

Figure 32 Odd-Shaped Asteroid.

be on the *Sky & Telescope* weekly "Skyline" phone message (see the "Sources of Information" section).

Another exciting kind of event is an asteroid occultation of a star. It is very difficult to predict exactly where these will occur in advance, but each year there may be a few at least remote chances for an observer at a given location. Observations of such events can give us information about the size and shape of the occulting asteroid and help further answer an odd question: Do asteroids have moons, or are they sometimes multiple bodies? In the 1970s, some occultation data made it look promising that there were asteroidal moons, but the years since have increased pessimism. Whatever you see of an asteroid occultation, your best way of finding out about them is through IOTA (International Occultation Timing Association—see the "Sources of Information" section). The finest upcoming events do get mentioned in the astronomy magazines (the January issue of *Sky & Telescope* always contains an IOTA look at the prospects for the year ahead).

One of the most outstanding attributes of the asteroids is simply that they are many. An excellent project for amateur astronomers is thus to try seeing as many of them as possible in a sky, in a night, in a year—and in a lifetime. Good opportunities to identify dim asteroids occur when one passes very close to an easily found star (these events are announced in the "Calendar Notes" of *Sky & Telescope's* "Celestial Calendar" section). Remember, however, that whether an asteroid is dim or bright, you should confirm that you have really seen it by detecting its motion over the course of at least two different nights.

There are now a few people—amateur astronomers—who have seen well over a thousand of the asteroids. Several thousand asteroids now have a name and number, although most of these have been discovered by photography and many have never been seen directly by the human eye.

Questions

1. Can you observe the Big Four asteroids and note at least the color of the brightest, Vesta and Ceres? Can you witness the brightness variations of asteroids like Eros?
2. Can you observe, when their approach is announced in time, some of the asteroids that pass very close to Earth? Can you look for asteroid occultations of stars?
3. How many and which asteroids can you see in a single sky, night, and year? How many and which in your lifetime?

53.

Telescopic Meteors

Observe some of our major meteor showers through the telescope for a while, especially if the telescopic peaks are on different nights than the naked-eye peaks. Make careful counts of the rates on these nights. Try counting the numbers of sporadic telescopic meteors on nonshower nights. Keep track of the brightest and dimmest meteors you ever see through the telescope. Note and try sketching from memory the details of meteors and their trails that you get to see in the telescope.

Meteors, popularly known as "shooting stars" or "falling stars," are streaks of light in the heavens that are really caused by pieces of space rock or iron that enter Earth's atmosphere at such high speeds that they burn up from friction. Such particles are rarely larger than grains of sand, even when they produce a very bright streak. Most are derived from comets; some, from asteroids—which are bigger than the biggest of meteoroids only by an arbitrary division in size. These objects are termed *meteoroids* in space, *meteors* in our atmosphere, and *meteorites* in the rare cases when they survive their fiery journey and reach the ground. They arrive in greater numbers from certain spots in the heavens on particular days each year in what are called *meteor showers.*

But these exciting objects—truly visitors from outer space and ancient pieces of the puzzle of the solar system—are usually looked for just with the naked eye. To see many bright ones, it is necessary to be able to survey a fairly large area of the heavens. And yet, despite the fact that meteor observing will always be mostly the province of the naked-eye observer, some interesting information can be learned from studying telescopic meteors.

Anyone who looks through the telescope frequently is startled from time to time by the sight of a telescopic meteor, which is usually rather faint even when seen with the added light-gathering power of a telescope. But what special features of the major meteor showers are observable through the telescope?

You might suppose that anyone who likes meteors would not wish to take away time from watching the naked-eye displays of a major shower. But it is possible to allot less-prime periods for the purpose; the peak of the telescopic meteors of a shower often comes days before or after the naked-eye peak; and anyone who likes meteors enough will want to explore new corners of the topic.

What follows here are some notes on telescopic meteor showers (cardinal directions refer to where they seem to come from as seen in mid-northern latitude skies).

1. The *Quadrantids* have a very brief period of good numbers. It is so brief that only observers in a limited range of longitudes on Earth have a shot at seeing a really great display of them each year. If this is not a year that your longitude is favored, consider that the telescopic peak occurs about 7 or 8 hours before the naked-eye peak. This indicates that the finer particles are located on the inner side of the Quadrantid stream of meteoroids. Both the naked-eye peak and the telescopic peak occur sometime on January 3 or 4. Check

186

the astronomy magazines, *Astronomical Calendar,* or *Meteor News* (see the "Sources of Information" section) for details each year. The *radiant*, the point in the heavens from which a meteor appears to come, of this shower is highest in the northeast just before dawn.

2. The *Eta Aquarids* are the dust from past returns of Halley's Comet that we encounter when we pass near the outbound part of the comet's orbit. The telescopic Eta Aquarids may peak around May 3, about 3 days before the naked-eye ones do. Look, as is usually a satisfactory strategy with meteors, a moderate distance away from the radiant (which is near the Water Jar of Aquarius). Time is the hour or two before morning twilight.

3. The *Ophiuchids.* On June 13, 1974, J. C. Bennett saw telescopic meteors coming from a radiant near the star Xi Ophiuchi.

4. The *Delta Aquarids* can produce near-maximum numbers for quite a few days around July 29. The shower is said to be particularly rich in telescopic meteors. Why not try looking for them on at least a few of the nights at well after midnight?

5. The *Perseids.* I have turned up no information on the telescopic Perseids. Perhaps there is much to learn about this aspect of our most popular meteor shower. Look for them around August 12.

6. The *Orionids* are the dust from past returns of Halley's Comet that we encounter when we pass near the inbound part of the comet's orbit. The telescopic Orionids supposedly peak about 1 day before the October 20–21 peak of the naked-eye shower. Look for them from the south in the last few hours before morning twilight.

7. The *Leonids* of November 17 and the *Geminids* of December 13 or 14 are two of our greatest showers. I have turned up nothing on their telescopic meteors. Thus, here is another fresh area for research.

Do not forget that a telescopic meteor must be coming from the radiant of the shower to be counted. How many meteors from other directions do you count? How many telescopic meteors are visible each hour on a nonshower night? See for yourself how many of these *sporadic* (nonshower) meteors you can see though the eyepiece. You can also note the brightest and the faintest meteors you ever see through the telescope. If you observe often enough with this purpose, you will eventually get to see some marvelous "close-up" detail in some meteors and their trails.

Questions

1. How many telescopic meteors can you see per hour from the major meteor showers? What is the peak night for their telescopic meteors?

2. How many sporadic telescopic meteors can you observe per hour on various shower and nonshower nights?

3. What are the brightest and the faintest meteors and trails you ever see through the telescope? What detail can you observe in some of them?

APPENDIXES

Appendix 1
Observational Data for the Planets

Planet	Min. Diam.*	Max. Diam.§	Mean Opp. Diam.**	Mean Opp. Mag.§§
Mercury	4.5	13.0	7.8***	0.0***
Venus	9.6	65.4	25.2***	−4.4***
Mars	3.5	25.7	17.9	−2.0
Jupiter	30.4	50.0	46.8	−2.7
Saturn	14.9	20.7	19.4	−0.2§§§
Uranus	3.3	4.1	3.9	+5.5
Neptune	2.1	2.3	2.3	+7.8
Pluto	—	—	—	+14

* Angular diameter in arc-seconds at greatest distance.

§ Angular diameter in arc-seconds at least distance.

** Angular diameter in arc-seconds at mean opposition distance.

§§ Visual magnitude at mean opposition distance.

*** At greatest elongation, not opposition.

§§§ With rings fully opened; magnitude +0.7 with rings closed.

Appendix 2
Greatest Elongations and Conjunctions with the Sun of Mercury and Venus, 1991–2000

MERCURY

1991	Elongs.:	Jan 14 (W), Mar 27 (E), May 12 (W), Jul 25 (E), Sep 7 (W), Nov 19 (E), Dec 27 (W)
	Conjs.:	Mar 2 (S), Apr 14 (I), Jun 17 (S), Aug 21 (I), Oct 3 (S), Dec 8 (I)
1992	Elongs.:	Mar 9 (E), Apr 23 (W), Jul 6 (E), Aug 21 (W), Oct 31 (E), Dec 9 (W)
	Conjs.:	Feb 12 (S), Mar 26 (I), May 31 (S), Aug 2 (I), Sep 15 (S), Nov 21 (I)
1993	Elongs.:	Feb 21 (E), Apr 5 (W), Jun 17 (E), Aug 4 (W), Oct 14 (E), Nov 22 (W)
	Conjs.:	Jan 23 (S), Mar 9 (I), May 16 (S), Jul 15 (I), Aug 29 (S), Nov 6 (I)
1994	Elongs.:	Feb 4 (E), Mar 19 (W), May 30 (E), Jul 17 (W), Sep 26 (E), Nov 6 (W)
	Conjs.:	Jan 3 (S), Feb 20 (I), Apr 30 (S), Jun 25 (I), Aug 13 (S), Oct 21 (I), Dec 14 (S)
1995	Elongs.:	Jan 19 (E), Mar 1 (W), May 12 (E), Jun 29 (W), Sep 9 (E), Oct 20 (W)
	Conjs.:	Feb 3 (I), Apr 14 (S), Jun 5 (I), Jul 28 (S), Oct 5 (I), Nov 23 (S)
1996	Elongs.:	Jan 2 (E), Feb 11 (W), Apr 23 (E), Jun 10 (W), Aug 21 (E), Oct 3 (W), Dec 15 (E)
	Conjs.:	Jan 18 (I), Mar 28 (S), May 15 (I), Jul 11 (S), Sep 17 (I), Nov 1 (S)
1997	Elongs.:	Jan 24 (W), Apr 6 (E), May 22 (W), Aug 4 (E), Sep 16 (W), Nov 28 (E)
	Conjs.:	Jan 2 (I), Mar 11 (S), Apr 25 (I), Jun 25 (S), Aug 31 (I), Oct 13 (S), Dec 17 (I)
1998	Elongs.:	Jan 6 (W), Mar 20 (E), May 4 (W), Jul 17 (E), Aug 31 (W), Nov 11 (E), Dec 20 (W)

	Conjs.:	Feb 22 (S), Apr 6 (I), Jun 10 (S), Aug 13 (I), Sep 25 (S), Dec 1 (I)
1999	Elongs.:	Mar 3 (E), Apr 16 (W), Jun 28 (E), Aug 14 (W), Oct 24 (E), Dec 3 (W)
	Conjs.:	Feb 4 (S), Mar 19 (I), May 25 (S), Jul 26 (I), Sep 8 (S), Nov 15 (I)
2000	Elongs.:	Feb 15 (E), Mar 28 (W), Jun 9 (E), Jul 27 (W), Oct 6 (E), Nov 15 (W)
	Conjs.:	Jan 16 (S), Mar 1 (I), May 9 (S), Jul 6 (I), Aug 22 (S), Oct 30 (I), Dec 25 (S)

VENUS

1991	Elongs.:	Jun 13 (E), Nov 2 (W)	1996	Elongs.:	Apr 1 (E), Aug 20 (W)
	Conjs.:	Aug 22 (I)		Conjs.:	Jun 10 (I)
1992	Elongs.:	None	1997	Elongs.:	Nov 6 (E)
	Conjs.:	Jun 13 (S)		Conjs.:	Apr 2 (S)
1993	Elongs.:	Jan 19 (E), Jun 10 (W)	1998	Elongs.:	Mar 27 (W)
	Conjs.:	Apr 1 (I)		Conjs.:	Jan 16 (I), Oct 30 (S)
1994	Elongs.:	Aug 24 (E)	1999	Elongs.:	Jun 11 (E), Oct 30 (W)
	Conjs.:	Jan 17 (S), Nov 2 (I)		Conjs.:	Aug 20 (I)
1995	Elongs.:	Jan 13 (W)	2000	Elongs.:	None
	Conjs.:	Aug 20 (S)		Conjs.:	Jun 11 (S)

E = eastern elongation; W = western elongation; I = inferior conjunction; S = superior conjunction.

Appendix 3
Oppositions of the Superior Planets, 1991–2000

Year	Mars	Jupiter	Saturn	Uranus	Neptune	Pluto
1991	None	Jan 28	Jul 27	Jul 4	Jul 8	May 10
1992	None	Feb 29	Aug 7	Jul 7	Jul 9	May 12
1993	Jan 7	Mar 30	Aug 19	Jul 12	Jul 12	May 14
1994	None	Apr 30	Sep 1	Jul 17	Jul 14	May 17
1995	Feb 12	Jun 1	Sep 14	Jul 21	Jul 17	May 20
1996	None	Jul 4	Sep 26	Jul 25	Jul 18	May 22
1997	Mar 17	Aug 9	Oct 10	Jul 29	Jul 21	May 25
1998	None	Sep 16	Oct 23	Aug 3	Jul 23	May 28
1999	Apr 24	Oct 23	Nov 6	Aug 7	Jul 26	May 31
2000	None	Nov 28	Nov 19	Aug 11	Jul 27	Jun 1

Appendix 4
Planetary Orbital Data and Synodic Periods

Planet	Mean Dist. (AU)	Sid. Per.*	Mean Syn. Per.§	Ecc.**	Orb. Inc.§§
Mercury	0.387	87.969d	115.88d	0.206	7.0°
Venus	0.723	224.701d	583.92d	0.007	3.4°
Earth	1.000	365.256d	—	0.017	0.0°
Mars	1.524	686.980d	779.94d	0.093	1.9°
Jupiter	5.203	11.862y	398.88d	0.048	1.3°
Saturn	9.539	29.457y	378.09d	0.056	2.5°
Uranus	19.182	84.010y	369.66d	0.047	0.8°
Neptune	30.058	164.793y	367.49d	0.009	1.8°
Pluto	39.44	248.5y	366.73d	0.25	17.1°

* Sidereal orbital period.
§ Mean synodic period.
** Orbital eccentricity.
§§ Inclination of orbit to ecliptic (plane of Earth's orbit).

Appendix 5
Physical Data for the Planets

Planet	Eq. Diam. (km)*	Mass	Volume	Mean Dens.§	Obl.**	Alb.§§
Mercury	4,878	0.06	0.06	5.43	0	0.11
Venus	12,104	0.82	0.86	5.24	0	0.65
Earth	12,756	1.00	1.00	5.52	0.0034	0.37
Mars	6,787	0.11	0.15	3.94	0.0052	0.15
Jupiter	142,800	317.83	1,323	1.33	0.065	0.52
Saturn	120,000	95.16	752	0.70	0.108	0.47
Uranus	50,800	14.50	64	1.30	0.030	0.51
Neptune	48,600	17.20	54	1.76	0.026	0.41
Pluto	2,250	0.002	0.01	c.2	0	c.0.3

* Equatorial diameter.
§ Mean density (density of water = 1).
** Oblateness.
§§ Albedo (0.0 = completely nonreflective; 1.0 = completely reflective).

Glossary

The entries that state "*See* Note . . ." refer to the "Note on the Measurement of Time, Position, Angular Distance, and Brightness in Astronomy."

Albedo: The reflectivity of astronomical objects.

Ansa (plural ansae): The part of a planetary ring system with the greatest apparent curvature, to either side of the planet.

Anti-tail: A comet tail that appears to point back toward the Sun.

Aperture effect: The reduction in perceived true coma size and total brightness with larger aperture (diameter of lens or mirror) in optical instruments.

Aphelion: Far point of an orbit around the Sun (opposite of *perihelion*).

Apogee: Far point of an orbit around Earth (opposite of *perigee*).

Apparition: Period of a planet's (or other object's) visibility between two periods when it is not viewable.

Ashen Light: Mysterious luminosity sometimes observed on the night side of Venus's disk.

Asteroids: Small worlds found mostly between the orbits of Mars and Jupiter (also called *minor planets*).

Astronomical unit (AU): The average distance between Earth and the Sun.

Aureole: The innermost area of scattered light around the Sun in our sky.

Baily's beads: Beads of the Sun's brilliant surface shining through lowland areas on the Moon's edge at the start or end of a total solar eclipse.

Belts: The planet-encircling bands of darker clouds on the gas giant planets.

Bipolar sunspot group: Group of sunspots that are related by being at the corresponding entrance and exit points of magnetic lines of force in a disturbance at the Sun's surface.

Celestial sphere: The imaginary sphere surrounding Earth whose inner surface is the sky above and below one's horizon.

Chromosphere: A colorful layer of the Sun's atmosphere glimpsed briefly at the start and end of a total solar eclipse.

Coma (of a comet): The cloud of gas and dust surrounding an active comet's *nucleus,* with the nucleus forming the comet's *head.*

Comet: A mass of frozen gas and dust (the nucleus) that releases this gas and dust to form a *coma* and (generally) a *tail* when exposed to sufficient solar radiation and heating.

Conjunction: Strictly speaking, the arrangement when one celestial object moves to a position due north or south of another; more loosely, any close pairing of celestial objects brought about by the motion of one or both.

Corona: The pearly white outer atmosphere of the Sun visible during total solar eclipses.

Cusp-caps: Caps of light occasionally observed on the points of the crescent Venus.

Danjon scale: A scale consisting of verbal descriptions for estimating the brightness of total lunar eclipses, invented by A. Danjon.

Delta effect: The failure of some comets to achieve as great a brightness and coma size as expected because their light is spread out too widely (and thus too thinly) when they are close to Earth.

Diamond-ring effect: The appearance at the start and end of some total solar eclipses of a first (or last) starlike point of the Sun's surface seen through a valley on the Moon's edge like a diamond on the band of the still-visible solar corona.

Dichotomy: A world's appearance of being precisely half lit (which does not occur at the time it theoretically should for Venus and Mercury because of Schroter's effect).

Earthshine: The glow from the sunlit parts of Earth seen on the night part of the Moon.

Eclipse: The hiding or dimming of one celestial object by another object or the other object's shadow.

Ecliptic: The apparent path of the Sun through the zodiac constellations, which is really the projection of Earth's orbit in the sky.

Egress: End of a transit or shadow transit.

Elongation: The angular separation of a celestial object from the Sun (rarely, the Moon or other body) in the sky.

Envelopes: Expanding clouds of dust or gas ejected in a comet's head (also called *halos*).

Evening Star: Venus (rarely, also Mercury) when it is east of the Sun and therefore visible in the evening sky.

Extended radius vector: The continuation of the imaginary line that runs from the Sun to a comet's nucleus.

Faculae: Brilliant regions of hydrogen floating above the solar surface that are best seen where they contrast with the less bright photosphere near the Sun's limb.

Gas giants: The planets whose gaseous atmospheres make up a sizable fraction of their entire bulk (Jupiter, Saturn, Uranus, and Neptune).

Greatest elongation: The maximum angular separation of an *inferior planet* from the Sun.

Inferior conjunction: Position in which an *inferior planet* passes the line between the Sun and Earth *(see also superior conjunction)*.

Inferior planet: A planet closer to the Sun than Earth is.

Ingress: Beginning of a transit or shadow transit.

Ion rays: Bright strands of ionized gas or plasma that are magnetic field line tracers in the *gas tail* (also called *ion* or *plasma tail*) of comets.

Jets: Gushers of dust or gas shooting out from active areas of a comet's nucleus.

Libration: Various kinds of tiltings of the face of the Moon pointed toward Earth.

Libration points: The *L-points* at which very small objects can have stable orbit in relation to two much more massive bodies (like the Earth and Moon or the Sun and Jupiter).

Light pollution: Excessive or misdirected lighting (generally manmade and outdoor).

Limb: The edge of a celestial body like the Sun or Moon.

Limiting magnitude: The faintest magnitude (level of brightness) at which celestial objects (usually stars) can be seen with a given set of sky conditions and optical instruments (including the naked eye).

Long-period comet: A comet with an orbital period of over 200 years (usually thousands or millions of years) probably seen only once in human history.

LTP (lunar transient phenomena): The mysterious ephemeral glows, flashes, colors, or darkenings that seem to occur occasionally at certain locations on the Moon.

Lunation: A cycle from one New Moon to the next New Moon.

Magnitude (as a measure of brightness): *See* "Note. . . ."

Magnitude (of an eclipse): The fraction of the Sun's diameter covered by the Moon or the fraction of the Moon's diameter covered by the Earth's shadow during eclipses (for total eclipses this fraction can be larger than 1).

Magnitude, absolute (of comets): The magnitude of a comet if it were 1 AU (astronomical unit) away from both the Sun and Earth.

Mare (plural maria): The gray plains of ancient lava on the Moon.

Meridian: The imaginary line from due north to overhead to due south in the sky.

Meteor: A "shooting star"; actually, the streak of light produced when a piece of rock or iron from space (where it is called a *meteoroid*) burns up from friction in the atmosphere on its way to vaporization or (in rare cases) reaching the ground (where it becomes a *meteorite*).

Meteor shower: An increased number of meteors seeming to come from a particular point in the heavens (if very intense, it can be called a *meteor storm*).

Minutes of arc: *See* "Note. . . ."

Morning Star: Venus (rarely, also Mercury) when it is west of the Sun and therefore visible in the morning (before sunrise) sky.

Nucleus (of a comet): The central body of dusty ice and rock in a comet.

Oblateness: Quality of having greater equatorial than polar width.

Occultation: The hiding of one celestial object by another (a *grazing occultation* is one in which the uneven edge of one body alternately hides and reveals the other).

Oort cloud: The vast swarm of innumerable pristine comet nuclei located well out beyond the orbits of the planets.

Opposition: Position opposite the Sun in the heavens, which is the most favorable for any superior planet.

Penumbra: Lighter, peripheral shadow (usually of Earth); lighter area of a sunspot.

Perigee: Near point of an orbit around Earth (opposite of *apogee*).

Perihelion: Near point of an orbit around the Sun (opposite of *aphelion*).

Periodic comet: A comet with an orbital period of less than 200 years that thus returns a number of times in human history or perhaps even in a human lifetime (also called *short-period comet*).

Phase effect: The trace of night side seen on the edge of a superior planet's disk as viewed from Earth (an effect at its greatest near quadrature).

Photosphere: Blindingly bright surface of the Sun.

Projection: Technique of casting an image of the Sun from an optical instrument or a pinhole onto a screen for easy and safe viewing.

Quadrature: Position of a planet 90° east or west of the Sun.

Radiant: Area of the heavens from which a meteor shower radiates.

Rays (on the Moon): Streaks of light-colored material ejected from craters on the Moon.

Relative Sunspot Number (RSN): A figure that conveys the amount of sunspot activity on the Sun, calculated from the number of sunspots and sunspot groups (by a method described in Activity 14).

Retrograde motion: Apparent backward (westward) movement of planets in front of the starry background (opposite of *direct motion*).

Right ascension (RA): *See* "Note. . . ."

Rills: Long cracklike features, often ravines, on the Moon.

Schroter's effect: The slight reduction of Venus's (and to a lesser extent Mercury's) phase due to the planet's departure from perfect, uniform smoothness.

Seconds of arc: *See* "Note. . . ."

"Seeing": Sharpness of astronomical images as a function of atmospheric turbulence.

Shadow transit: Passage of a moon's shadow across the face of a planet.

Short-period comet: *See periodic comet.*

Sidereal month: The period required for the Moon to make one circuit around Earth and return to the same point as seen against the stars.

Skyglow: Illumination of the sky by terrestrial sources (almost always manmade sources, usually cities).

Solar wind: The ceaseless (but varying) outflow of atomic particles from the Sun.

Sporadic meteor: A meteor not belonging to any known shower.

198

Stationary point: Point at which a planet halts apparent motion in the heavens when switching from direct to retrograde motion (or back to direct).

Strip sketch: A drawing of all the features of a planet seen along a latitudinal band for the range of longitudes properly observed during the course of a protracted viewing session.

Sun-picture: A projected image of the Sun.

Sunspot: A darker, cooler (actually only somewhat less blindingly bright and hot) region on the Sun.

Superior conjunction: Position in which an *inferior planet* passes the extension of the Sun–Earth line on the far side of the Sun from Earth (*see also inferior conjunction*).

Superior planet: A planet farther out from the Sun than Earth is.

Synodic month: The period required for the Moon to go from one phase to next recurrence of this phase (same Sun–Earth–Moon relation).

Synodic period: The period of time it takes for a planet to return to the same position with respect to Earth and the Sun.

Terminator: The line separating day and night on a world.

Transit: Passage of a planet in front of the Sun or passage of a moon in front of a planet.

Transparency: Quality of the atmosphere's ability to pass amount of light (in other words, clarity of the air).

Umbra: Central, darker shadow of any object (especially Earth); darker part of a sunspot.

Violet clearing: Occasional (and unexplained) episode of unusual transparency of Mars's atmosphere to violet light.

Wave of darkening: Episode of apparent darkening of dark Martian surface features (proven to be actually a brightening of the light areas, which makes the dark features more prominent).

W-clouds: Orographic (mountain-caused) clouds on Mars, especially those forming a W-shape in the Tharsis region.

Zenith: The overhead point in the sky.

Zodiac: The band of constellations in which the Sun, Moon, and planets are found and whose midline is the *ecliptic.*

Zones: The planet-encircling bands of lighter clouds on the gas giant planets.

Sources of Information

Association of Lunar and Planetary Observers (ALPO)

ALPO is the great international organization for amateur observers of solar system bodies. The journal of ALPO, better known as *The Strolling Astronomer,* is published quarterly. The organization has about a dozen "sections" devoted to particular worlds or classes of bodies; some of the sections have further subdivisions and more than one "recorder" (expert director). ALPO also offers a number of handbooks and newsletters. To learn about these, *The Strolling Astronomer,* the sections, and membership in the organization, write to the overall director of ALPO, John Westfall, P.O. Box 16131, San Francisco, CA 94116.

Books

Some of the following works are out of print at present but are worth looking up at your library or ordering through interlibrary loan. Remember also that in each of the categories, ALPO has interesting books of its own to offer.

General

Beatty, J. Kelly, and Andrew Chaikin. *The New Solar System* (Third Edition, 1990). New York: Cambridge University Press; and Cambridge, MA: Sky Publishing Corporation.

Briggs, G. A., and F. W. Taylor. *The Cambridge Photographic Atlas of the Planets.* New York: Cambridge University Press.

Ley, Willy. *Watchers of the Skies.* New York: Viking Press. World-by-world histories of observing the planets and other solar system bodies.

Littmann, Mark. *Planets Beyond—Discovering the Outer Solar System.* New York: John Wiley & Sons.

Meeus, Jean. *Astronomical Tables of the Sun, Moon, and Planets.* Willmann-Bell, Inc., P.O. Box 3125, Richmond, VA 23235.

Miller, Ron, and William K. Hartmann. *The Grand Tour—A Traveler's Guide to the Solar System.* New York: Workman Publishing.

Moore, Patrick. *The New Guide to the Planets.* New York: W.W. Norton.

Ottewell, Guy. *The Astronomical Companion.* Astronomical Workshop, Furman University, Greenville, SC 29613. Illuminating diagrams and explanations of Sun, Moon, eclipses, meteors, comets, and much more.

Schaaf, Fred. *The Starry Room.* New York: John Wiley & Sons. Essays on eclipses, meteors, comets, and other topics.

Sun and Moon

Alter, Dinsmore. *Pictorial Guide to the Moon.* New York: Crowell.

Mitton, Simon. *Daytime Star.* New York: Scribner's.

Moore, Patrick. *New Guide to the Moon.* New York: W.W. Norton.

Price, Fred W. *The Moon Observer's Handbook.* New York: Cambridge University Press.

Particular Planets

Alexander, A. F. O'D. *The Planet Saturn.* London: Faber & Faber.

Hunt, G., and Patrick Moore. *The Planet Venus.* London: Faber & Faber.

Miles, Frank, and Nicholas Booth. *Race to Mars.* New York: Harper & Row.

Peek, Bertrand. *The Planet Jupiter—The Observer's Handbook.* London: Faber & Faber.

Comets, Asteroids, and Meteors

Chapman, Robert D., and John C. Brandt. *The Comet Book.* Boston: Jones & Bartlett Publishers, Inc.

Cunningham, Clifford J. *Introduction to Asteroids.* Willmann-Bell, Inc., P.O. Box 3125, Richmond, VA 23235.

Ottewell, Guy, and Fred Schaaf. *Mankind's Comet.* Astronomical Workshop, Furman University, Greenville, SC 29613. The most comprehensive book on Halley's Comet (including its past and future) but also contains large sections on comets in general and on comet observing.

Roggemans, Paul, editor. *Handbook for Visual Meteor Observations.* Cambridge, MA: Sky Publishing Corporation.

Seargent, David. *Comets: Vagabonds of Space.* New York: Doubleday.

Observing Manuals

Dobbins, Thomas, Donald C. Parker, and Charles F. Capen. *Introduction to Observing and Photographing the Solar System.* Willmann-Bell, Inc., P.O. Box 3125, Richmond, VA 23235.

Muirden, James. *The Amateur Astronomer's Handbook.* New York: Harper & Row.

Norton's 2000.0 Star Atlas and Reference Handbook. Ian Ridpath, editor. New York: Longman Scientific & Technical and John Wiley & Sons.

Sherrod, P. Clay. *A Complete Manual of Amateur Astronomy.* New York: Prentice-Hall.

Telescopes

Brown, Sam. *All About Telescopes.* Edmund Scientific Company, 101 East Gloucester Pike, Barrington, NJ 08007. Outdated in places but very user-friendly with clear text and innumerable diagrams.

Muirden, James. *How to Use An Astronomical Telescope.* New York: Simon & Schuster.

Rutten, H., and M. van Venrooij. *Telescope Optics—Evaluation and Design.* Willmann-Bell, Inc., P.O. Box 3125, Richmond, VA 23235.

Periodicals

In addition to the following publications, check your library for the professional journal of solar system studies, *Icarus.*

Astronomy. Kalmbach Publishing Company, 21027 Crossroads Circle, P.O. Box 1612, Waukesha, WI 53187. General astronomy magazine.

Mercury. Astronomical Society of the Pacific, 390 Ashton Avenue, San Francisco, CA 94112. The title does not mean that the magazine is devoted to only the planet Mercury; the full range of astronomy topics is covered.

Meteor News. Route 3, Box 1062, Callahan, FL 32011.

Sky & Telescope. Sky Publishing Corporation, P.O. Box 9111, Belmont, MA 02178. General astronomy magazine.

Sky Calendar. Abrams Planetarium, Michigan State University, East Lansing, MI 48824.

News Services and Irregular Bulletins

Comet Rapid Announcement Service. CRAS, P.O. Box 110282, Cleveland, OH 44111. A publication (free until recently) containing detailed finder charts and other information for new comets.

Skyline. Recorded telephone message, updated weekly (sometimes more often), by *Sky & Telescope* magazine (see address given under "Periodicals"). Gives comet discoveries and positions, notification of Martian dust storms, and much else. Phone number: (617)497-4168.

W. R. Brooks Observatory Comet Circulars. R.R. #1, Box 198, Gold Road, Stormville, NY 12582. Notifies you of comet discoveries and predicted positions of notable comets. Wise discussion of each object by comet expert John Bortle.

Annuals

Astronomical Almanac. U.S. Naval Observatory, 34th and Massachusetts Avenue, NW, Washington, D.C. 20392. The standard reference of this kind.

Astronomical Calendar. Atlas-size guide by Guy Ottewell. Astronomical Workshop, Furman University, Greenville, SC 29613.

Observer's Handbook. Toronto: Royal Astronomical Society of Canada.

Maps, Audiovisual Aids, and Other Educational Materials

Astronomical Society of the Pacific. 300 Ashton Avenue, San Francisco, CA 94112. This organization offers photographs, slide sets, video- and audiotapes, plus books and more.

Sky Publishing Corporation. P.O. Box 9111, Belmont, MA 02178. Among many other publications, this corporation provides lunar and planetary maps and ESSCO classroom publications (including laboratory exercises in astronomy).

General Index

Crater Index

Other craters are mentioned in the list of those near limb (p. 31); other references to many of the craters given below and some other craters occur in the annotated list of selected craters on pp. 17–21. Most of the craters given below, plus many others, are named on the maps of Figures 2, 3, 4, and 5.